092125

WITHDRAWN

D0773384

Primary Space Project Research Team

Research Co-ordinating Group

Professor Paul Black (Co-director)
Jonathan Osborne

Professor Wynne Harlen (Co-director)[1]
Terry Russell

Centre for Educational Studies
King's College London
University of London
Cornwall House Annexe
Waterloo Road
London SE1 8TX

Centre for Research in Primary Science
and Technology
Department of Education
University of Liverpool
126 Mount Pleasant
Liverpool L3 5SR

Tel: 071-872-3094

Tel: 051-794 3270

Project Researchers

Pamela Wadsworth (from 1989)

Derek Bell (from 1989)
Ken Longden (from 1989)
Adrian Hughes (1989)
Linda McGuigan (from 1989)
Dorothy Watt (1986-89)

Associated Researchers

John Meadows
(South Bank University)

Bert Sorsby
John Entwistle
(Edge Hill College)

LEA Advisory Teachers

Maureen Smith (1986-89)
(ILEA)

Joan Boaden
Karen Hartley
Kevin Cooney (1986-88)
(Knowsley)

Joyce Knaggs (1986-88)
Heather Scott (from 1989)
Ruth Morton (from 1989)
(Lancashire)

---

[1] Now Director of the Scottish Council for Research in Education, 15 St John St, Edinburgh, EH8 8JR

PRIMARY SPACE PROJECT
RESEARCH REPORT

January 1994

The Earth in Space

by
**Jonathan Osborne, Pam Wadsworth,
Paul Black and John Meadows**

LIVERPOOL UNIVERSITY PRESS

First published 1994 by
Liverpool University Press
PO Box 147, Liverpool, L69 3BX

Copyright © 1994 Liverpool King's SPACE Project

All rights reserved. No part of this book may be
reproduced, stored in a retrieval system, or
transmitted, in any form or by any means,
electronic, mechanical, photocopying, recording,
or otherwise, without the prior written permission
of the copyright owner.

British Library Cataloguing-in-Publication Data
A British Library CIP Record is available

ISBN 0 85323 008 0

Printed and bound in the European Community by
Redwood Books, Trowbridge, Wiltshire

CONTENTS

INTRODUCTION

This introduction provides an overview of the SPACE Project and its programme of research.

The Primary SPACE Project is a classroom-based research project which aims to establish

- *the ideas which primary school children have in particular science concept areas.*

- *the possibility of children modifying their ideas as the result of relevant experiences.*

The research is funded by the Nuffield Foundation and the publishers, Collins Educational, and is being conducted at two centres, the Centre for Research in Primary Science and Technology, Department of Education, University of Liverpool and the Centre for Educational Studies, King's College, London. The joint directors are Doctor Wynne Harlen and Professor Paul Black. The following local education authorities have been involved: Inner London Education Authority, Knowsley and Lancashire.

The Project is based on the view that children develop their ideas through the experiences they have. With this in mind, the Project has two main aims: firstly, to establish (through an elicitation phase) what specific ideas children have developed and what experiences might have led children to hold these views; and secondly, to see whether, within a normal classroom environment, it is possible to encourage a change in the ideas in a direction which will help children develop a more 'scientific' understanding of the topic (the intervention phase).

In the first phase of the Project from 1987 to 1989 eight concept areas were studied:

Electricity
Evaporation and condensation
Everyday changes in non-living materials
Forces and their effect on movement
Growth
Light
Living things' sensitivity to their environment
Sound

In the second phase of the Project during 1989 and 1990, a further ten concept areas were studied:

Earth
Earth in space
Energy
Genetics and evolution
Human influences on the Earth
Processes of life
Seasonal changes
Types and uses of materials
Variety of Life
Weather

Research Reports are usually based on each of these concept areas; occasionally where the areas are closely linked, they have been combined in a single report.

The Project has been run collaboratively between the University research teams, local education authorities and schools, with the participating teachers playing an active role in the development of the Project work.

Over the life-span of the Project a close relationship has been established between the University researchers and teachers, resulting in the development of techniques which advance both classroom practice and research. These methods provide opportunities, within the classroom, for children to express their ideas and to develop their thinking with the guidance of the teacher, and also help researchers towards a better understanding of children's thinking.

The Involvement of the Teachers

Schools and teachers were not selected for the Project on the basis of a particular background or expertise in primary science. In the majority of cases, two teachers per school were involved. This was advantageous in providing mutual support. Where possible, the Authority provided supply cover for the teachers so that they could attend Project sessions for preparation, training and discussion during the school day. Sessions were also held in the teachers' own time, after school.

The Project team aimed to have as much contact as possible with the teachers throughout the work to facilitate the provision of both training and support. The diversity of experience and differences in teaching style which the teachers brought with them to the Project meant that achieving a uniform style of presentation in all classrooms would not have been possible, or even desirable. Teachers were encouraged to incorporate the Project work into their existing classroom organisation so that both they and the children were as much at ease with the work as with any other classroom experience.

The Involvement of Children

The Project involved a cross-section of classes of children throughout the primary age range. A large component of the Project work was classroom-based, and all of the children in the participating classes were involved as far as possible. Small groups of children and individuals were selected for additional activities or interviews to facilitate more detailed discussion of their thinking.

The Structure of the Project

In the first phase of the Project, for each of the concept areas studied, a list of concepts was compiled to be used by researchers as the basis for the development of work in that area. These lists were drawn up from the standpoint of accepted scientific understanding and contained concepts which were considered to be a necessary part of a scientific understanding of each topic. The lists were not necessarily considered to be statements of the understanding which would be desirable in a child at age eleven, at the end of the Primary phase of schooling. The concept lists defined and outlined the area of interest for each of the studies; what ideas children were able to develop was a matter for empirical investigation.

In the second phase of the Project, the delineation of the concept area was informed by the National Curriculum for Science in England and Wales. The concept area was broken into a number of themes from which issues were selected for research. Themes sometimes contained a number of interlocking concepts; in other instances, they reflected only one underlying principle.

Most of the Project research work can be regarded as being organised into two major phases each followed by the collection of structured data about children's ideas. These phases called 'Exploration' and 'Intervention', are described in the following paragraphs and together with the data collection produce the following pattern for the research.

Phase 1a	*Exploration*
Phase 1b	*Pre-Intervention Elicitation*
Phase 2a	*Intervention*
Phase 2b	*Post-Intervention Elicitation*

The Phases of the Research

For the first eight concept areas, the above phases were preceded by an extensive pilot phase. Each phase, particularly the pilot work, was regarded as developmental; techniques and procedures were modified in the light of experience. The modifications involved a refinement of both the exposure materials and the techniques used to elicit ideas. This flexibility allowed the Project team to respond to unexpected situations and to incorporate useful developments into the programme.

Pilot Phase

There were three main aims of the pilot phase. They were, firstly to trial the techniques used to establish children's ideas, secondly, to establish the range of ideas held by primary school children, and thirdly, to familiarise the teachers with the classroom techniques being employed by the Project. This third aim was very important since teachers were being asked to operate in a manner which, to many of them, was very different from their usual style. By allowing teachers a 'practice run', their initial apprehensions were reduced, and the Project rationale became more familiar. In other words, teachers were being given the opportunity to incorporate Project techniques into their teaching, rather than having them imposed upon them.

Once teachers had become used to the SPACE way of working, a pilot phase was no longer essential and it was not always used when tackling the second group of concept areas. Moreover, teachers had become familiar with both research methodology and classroom techniques, having been involved in both of them. The pace of research could thus be quickened. Whereas pilot, exploration and intervention had extended over two or three terms, research in each concept area was now reduced to a single term.

In the Exploration phase children engaged with activities set up in the classroom for them to use, without any direct teaching. The activities were designed to ensure that a range of fairly common experiences (with which children might well be familiar from their everyday lives) was uniformly accessible to all children to provide a focus for their thoughts. In this way, the classroom activities were to help children articulate existing ideas rather than to provide them with novel experiences which would need to be interpreted.

Each of the topics studied raised some unique issues of technique and these distinctions led to the Exploration phase receiving differential emphasis. Topics in which the central concepts involved long-term, gradual changes, such as 'Growth', necessitated the incorporation of a lengthy exposure period in the study. A much shorter period of exposure, directly prior to elicitation was used with topics such as 'Light' and 'Electricity' which involve 'instant' changes.

During the Exploration teachers were encouraged to collect their children's ideas using informal classroom techniques. These techniques were:

i **Using Log-Books (free writing/drawing)**
Where the concept area involved long-term changes, it was suggested that children should make regular observations of the materials, with the frequency of these depending on the rate of change. The log-books could be pictorial or written, depending on the age of the children involved, and any entries could be supplemented by teacher comment if the children's thoughts needed explaining more fully. The main purposes of these log-books were to focus attention on the activities and to provide an informal record of the children's observations and ideas.

ii **Structured Writing/Annotated Drawing**
Writing or drawings produced in response to a particular question were extremely informative. Drawings and diagrams were particularly revealing when children added their own words to them. The annotation helped to clarify the ideas that a drawing represented.

Teachers also asked children to clarify their diagrams and themselves added explanatory notes and comments where necessary, after seeking clarification from children. Teachers were encouraged to note down any comments which emerged during dialogue, rather than ask children to write them down themselves. It was felt that this technique would remove a pressure from children which might otherwise have inhibited the expression of their thoughts.

iii **Completing a Picture**
Children were asked to add the relevant points to a picture. This technique ensured that children answered the questions posed by the Project team and reduced the possible effects of competence in drawing skills on ease of expression of ideas. The structured drawings provided valuable opportunities for teachers to talk to individual children and to build up a picture of each child's understanding.

iv **Individual Discussion**
It was suggested that teachers use an open-ended questioning style with their children. The value of listening to what children said, and of respecting their responses, was emphasised as was the importance of clarifying the meaning of words children used. This style of questioning caused some teachers to be

concerned that, by accepting any response whether right or wrong, they might implicitly be reinforcing incorrect ideas. The notion of ideas being acceptable and yet provisional until tested was at the heart of the Project. Where this philosophy was a novelty, some conflict was understandable.

In the Elicitation which followed Exploration, the Project team collected structured data through individual interviews and work with small groups. The individual interviews were held with a random, stratified sample of children to establish the frequencies of ideas held. The same sample of children was interviewed pre- and post-Intervention so that any shifts in ideas could be identified.

Intervention Phase

The Elicitation phase produced a wealth of different ideas from children, and produced some tentative insights into experiences which could have led to the genesis of some of these ideas. During the Intervention, teachers used this information as a starting point for classroom activities, or interventions, which were intended to lead to children extending their ideas. In schools where a significant level of teacher involvement was possible, teachers were provided with a general framework to guide their structuring of classroom activities appropriate to their class. Where opportunities for exposing teachers to Project techniques had been more limited, teachers were given a package of activities which had been developed by the Project team.

Both the framework and the Intervention activities were developed as a result of preliminary analysis of the Pre-Intervention Elicitation data. The Intervention strategies were:

(a) **Encouraging children to test their ideas.**
It was felt that, if pupils were provided with the opportunity to test their ideas in a scientific way, they might find some of their ideas to be unsatisfying. This might encourage the children to develop their thinking in a way compatible with greater scientific competence.

(b) **Encouraging children to develop more specific definitions for particular key words.**
Teachers asked children to make collections of objects which exemplified particular words, thus enabling children to define words in a relevant context, through using them.

(c) **Encouraging children to generalise from one specific context to others through discussion.**
Many ideas which children held appeared to be context-specific. Teachers provided children with opportunities to share ideas and experiences so that they might be enabled to broaden the range of contexts in which their ideas applied.

(d) **Finding ways to make imperceptible changes perceptible.**
Long-term, gradual changes in objects which could not readily be perceived were problematic for many children. Teachers endeavoured to find appropriate ways of making these changes perceptible. For example, the fact that a liquid could 'disappear' visually yet still be sensed by the sense of smell - as in the

case of perfume - might make the concept of evaporation more accessible to children.

(e) **Testing the 'right' idea alongside the children's own ideas.**
Children were given activities which involved solving a problem. To complete the activity, a scientific idea had to be applied correctly, thus challenging the child's notion. This confrontation might help children to develop a more scientific idea.

(f) **Using secondary sources.**
In many cases, ideas were not testable by direct practical investigation. It was, however, possible for children's ideas to be turned into enquiries which could be directed at books or other secondary sources of information.

(g) **Discussion with others.**
The exchange of ideas with others could encourage individuals to reconsider their own ideas. Teachers were encouraged to provide contexts in which children could share and compare their ideas.

In the Post-Intervention Elicitation phase the Project team collected a complementary set of data to that from the Pre-Intervention Elicitation by re-interviewing the same sample of children. The data were analysed to identify changes in ideas across the sample as a whole and also in individual children.

These phases of Project work form a coherent package which provides opportunities for children to explore and develop their scientific understanding as a part of classroom activity, and enables researchers to come nearer to establishing what conceptual development it is possible to encourage within the classroom and the most effective strategies for its encouragement.

The Implications of the Research

The SPACE Project has developed a programme which has raised many issues in addition to those of identifying and changing children's ideas in a classroom context. The question of teacher and pupil involvement in such work has become an important part of the Project, and the acknowledgement of the complex interactions inherent in the classroom has led to findings which report changes in teacher and pupil attitudes as well as in ideas. Consequently, the central core of activity, with its data collection to establish changes in ideas should be viewed as just one of the several kinds of change upon which the efficacy of the Project must be judged.

The following pages provide a detailed account of the development of the Earth in Space topic, the Project findings and the implications which they raise for science education.

The research reported in this and the companion research reports, as well as being of intrinsic interest, informed the writing and development with teachers of the Primary SPACE Project curriculum materials, to be published by Collins Educational.

1. Previous Research - A Review

The attractions of studying children's astronomical thinking are several and various. Just as astronomy was the earliest domain for scientific theorising, it represents one of the first areas of scientific thought where children are asked to transcend their concrete experiences and the logic of commonsense, for instance, the natural intuition that the Sun goes around the Earth. Instead they are expected to accept the seemingly less rational, and less justifiable arguments that it is the Earth that spins and that people on the other side of the Earth do not fall off. Thus any research not only reveals children's domain specific reasoning, but how their thinking adapts and changes to the scientific world view (or not); thus some researchers have been attracted to this domain to study the development in children's thinking.

The earliest research in this domain was undertaken by Piaget (1929) to explore the growth and development of children's knowledge and epistemology. One chapter of his work, *The Child's Conception of the World,* is devoted to children's explanations for the behaviour of the Sun and Moon. Piaget's particular interest was the child's ontology and understanding of causality.

Only in the last two decades has the topic attracted much attention again, principally from those researchers interested in children's alternative frameworks. These later studies have explored the child's conception of the Earth (Nussbaum & Novak, 1976; Nussbaum, 1979; Mali & Howe, 1979; Sneider & Pulos, 1983; Vosniadou, 1991), or alternatively, looked more broadly at children's knowledge and understanding of a variety of other topics e.g. their explanations for the rotation of the Earth, night and day and their estimates the relative sizes of the Moon, Earth and Sun (Klein, 1982; Jones, Lynch & Reesink, 1987; Baxter, 1989; Vosniadou, 1991).

For both groups of researchers, the principal attraction of the area has been the question of how the child comes to construct and use astronomical models which are counter-intuitive. Historically, the phylogenetic origins of the scientific conception of the Earth and its movement through the heavens led to some of the most well-known conflicts between individuals and the establishment. However, since photographs now provide incontrovertible evidence that the Earth is a sphere, it cannot be argued that the development of children's thinking follows the historical development of ideas. So how does the child now shift from the naive 'flat earth' conception to the scientific world view? The work of the first group of researchers has led to the elaboration of a set of categorical descriptions of the development of children's thinking which describe a possible sequence of progression and which differ from the work of Piaget in terms of the scope of and the sequence of the growth of the child's knowledge and understanding which they propose.

From the perspective of cognitive psychology the more fundamental question is whether the child's knowledge can be characterised in terms of elements of fragmented and unrelated knowledge, or alternatively, does the child hold a coherent theory? Secondly is any change dependent simply on the accretion of more information which leads to some minor or weak restructuring of their ideas or alternatively, are children operating with internally consistent naive theories which require radical restructuring to achieve scientific understanding?

Children's Explanations

Nearly all researchers have used the clinical interview to explore children's thinking and from an analysis of the responses developed a schema which they have argued reflects progression in children's thinking. Whilst there are differences between these schema, it is possible to see commonalities. Piaget asked young children a series of questions such as 'How did the Sun begin?', 'What is the Moon like?', 'Why is there only half of it?' etc. Later researchers tended to use more specific questions based on the use of models or representational drawings so that part of the difference in their conclusions can undoubtedly be attributed to the differing methodologies.

From a thorough and systematic analysis of their responses, Piaget proposed a three stage model of the development in children's thinking. In the first stage children may say that the Sun and the Moon are made or produced by human or divine agents. Such explanations he characterised as 'artificialism', arguing that explanations of this type are generally a mixture of the 'artificial' where origin is ascribed to the intervention of an external agency, and the animistic where the objects themselves are given properties of life, consciousness and will. Many examples are provided by Piaget e.g

> Caud (9;4)[1] : "How did the Sun start? ---*With heat.* --- What heat? ---*From the fire.* ----Where is the fire? --- *In heaven.* --- How did it start? ---*God lit it with coal and wood.*"

---

[1]   These figures give the age of the child in years and months respectively

In the second stage of development, children's explanations for the origin of natural phenomena display aspects which are half natural, in that they are simply descriptive, and half 'artificial'. For instance, in the following example the child provides a natural explanation for the origin of the Sun and an 'artificial' explanation for the origin of the mountain.

> Font (6;9) "Where does the Sun come from? --- *from the mountain.............* And how did the mountain begin? --- *it was people who made it."*

In the third and final stage, he argued that children's explanations shows that the origins of the Sun and the Moon are unrelated to human action.

> Aud (9;8) " What is the Sun made of? --- *Of clouds.* --- How did the Sun begin? --- *To begin with it was a ball and then it caught fire."*

Piaget argued that children's explanation of day and night followed a similar sequence though he added an additional intermediate stage.

In stage 1, sleep is the precursor and cause of night and the child is essentially unconcerned with 'how'. Piaget defines this as precausality because the child never seeks to explain 'how' the phenomenon occurs but simply 'why', ascribing causality to the underlying purpose i.e. it gets dark because we need to go to sleep. In his second stage, precausality remains but an explanation of the question 'how' has now been found. For example, night is seen as caused by a big, black cloud. The cloud does not block out the day and is not a screen - it is night itself derived from black air. In the third stage night is defined as a shadow produced by clouds blocking the daylight. Finally in the fourth stage, the children realise that night results solely from the Sun's disappearance though this does not imply that they know that the Earth spins on its axis. Children's progression was portrayed as a decrease in artificialism at the expense of a progressive search for explanations which identify causal elements (air, smoke, clouds, water) to account for the phenomena.

Jones, Lynch & Reesink (1987) identified five different explanations provided by children for the Earth-Sun-Moon system in terms of the shape, size and motion of these components.

Model 1   The Earth is stationary at the centre (geocentric). The Sun comes from nowhere in the morning and goes away at the end of the day.

Model 2   The Earth is stationary at the centre (geocentric) but spins. The Moon and Sun remain stationary.

Model 3   The Earth is stationary at the centre. The Sun and Moon rotate around the Earth.

Model 4   This is a heliocentric model. The Earth and Moon orbit around the Sun on concentric or the same orbits. With this model, children can correctly explain a range of phenomena but it is not the scientific model.

Model 5   The scientific understanding with the Earth orbiting the Sun and the Moon orbiting the Earth.

Only the first of these models bears any similarity to Piaget's findings but their work can be seen as extending Piaget's fourth stage. Their approach was to use clinical interviews based around a set of shapes of different sizes (spheres, hemispheres, circular discs, cylindrical rods, semi-circular discs, circles and semi-circles) with a sample of 32 Australian children from the third and sixth grade[2]. Children were asked to pick the shapes that most resembled the shape of the astronomical object being discussed and to use their shapes to model the movements of the Sun, Moon and Earth during one day.

They point out that, of these 5 models, the latter four have their own internal logic and will successfully explain day and night. They also suggest that they may form a hierarchy which represents children's progression. Applying a binary division into geocentric models (1-3) and heliocentric models (4 & 5), they found that children of age 11/12 were more likely to choose the latter and argued that this result reflects a progression in children's understanding. Their analysis of the chosen shapes showed that the grade 6 children were significantly more likely to choose the correct shape for the Sun, Moon and Earth, but that there was no relationship between pupil age and choice of an object of the correct relative size.

The schema produced by Baxter (1989) for children's explanations of day and night, from a questionnaire elaborates a set of six levels of explanation which are essentially a synthesis of the earlier work of Piaget and Jones et al. Table 1.1 show the percentage of children at age 9/10 holding each model.

Only a minority of children of this age have assimilated the scientific view and what is notable about his data is that, by the age of 15/16, it was still only a minority (47%)

---

[2]   These children would be age 8/9 and 11/12 respectively

who gave the scientific, heliocentric explanation for day and night which is indicative of the strength and tenacity of intuitive explanations.

Model	Percentage[3] %
Sun goes behind the hill	0.3
Clouds cover the Sun	9.0
Moon covers the Sun	9.6
Sun goes around the Earth once a day	16.4
Earth goes around the Sun once a day	45.8
Earth spins on its axis once a day	18.9

Table 1.1: Percentage of children age 9/10 selecting each type of explanation for the occurrence of day & night.

More recent work by Vosniadou (1991) categorised the children's explanations (age 5-11) that she obtained into 12 distinct types. However, many of these are refinements of the broad categories proposed by Piaget, Jones et al and Baxter. Consequently, the following summary is offered as a synthesis which would broadly summarise all of these findings of children's explanations for day and night and may represent a developmental sequence.

	Explanation	*Explanatory schema*
Model 1	Artificialistic explanations e.g. God makes it do that.	*Pre-causal thinking. Objects are purposive and actions are caused by external agencies.*
Model 2	Intuitive explanations and naturalistic explanations e.g the Sun goes away, clouds cover the Sun, the Moon goes behind the Sun.	*Explanation based on natural motions.*

---

[3]   Baxter does not give actual figures for his data, but presents it in the form of a bar chart from which the percentages have been calculated.

Model 3	Earth is stationary and the Sun goes around the Earth once a day.	*Explanations based on natural motions. The geocentric argument.*
Model 4	The Earth goes around the Sun once a day.	*Accommodation to the scientific explanation.*
Model 5	The Earth spins on its axis once a day.	*Scientific thinking.*

A similar but more general schema has been suggested by Finegold & Pundak (1991) who devised a questionnaire to assess children's (age 6-18) position within their sequence.

The Child's conception of the Earth

Probably one of the most seminal pieces of work in this domain is that undertaken by Nussbaum and Novak (1976). Their data were collected from a set of clinical interviews of 52 second grade, American schoolchildren. These children were asked questions about the shape of the Earth, the direction they would have to look in order to see the Earth and to predict the direction of fall of an object held by an individual located at different points on the Earth. Further questions were then used to explore the children's responses. From their data, they established a set of five notions or concepts which children commonly held about the Earth. These were defined as:-

Notion 1: The Earth we live on is flat and not like a round ball. Children holding this idea did not explicitly state that the Earth is flat, but verbal probing revealed that they did not believe that we live on the surface of a large sphere. A commonly held idea is that there are two Earths, the one we live on and a spherical ball which is in the sky. This may be due to the association of spherical globes with the Moon and the Sun in the sky.

Notion 2: Children who hold this idea will state that we live on a spherical ball and suggest proofs of this idea such as travelling around it or viewing it from space. However, such children believed that objects would fall off the Earth from anywhere in the Southern Hemisphere and did not differ substantially from children who hold notion 1. When their belief was forced into conflict with their immediate sense perception, their commitment to the notion of a round Earth was revealed as weak.

Notion 3: Whilst the thinking of such children was substantively similar to that of notion 2, the crucial difference was in explaining what would happen to water in a bottle located at the south pole. When asked 'Where would the water fall to?', notion 2 children said it would fall to the ground beneath whereas notion 3 children said that it would fall to the sky. Hence such children saw the Earth as being surrounded by the sky.

Notion 4: Here the idea is held that we live on a spherical planet and use the Earth as a frame of reference for up-down. However, children with this idea still showed some confusion in explaining in which direction an object would fall when dropped into the ground down mineshafts. That is, they had not fully internalised the concept of 'down' as the direction of the centre of the Earth.

Notion 5: Children who held this notion demonstrated a satisfactory and stable notion of the Earth as a planet which is a) spherical, b) surrounded by space and c) one where objects fall to the centre.

Further work by Nussbaum (1979) lead to the refinement of this schema. Notion 1 and 2 were conjoined and a new notion 2 introduced. In this notion, children saw people living *in* a huge ball composed of two hemispheres. They live on the horizontal plane in the bottom hemisphere and the top hemisphere is not solid. For the first time though, the Earth is seen as a finite body surrounded by space and Nussbaum argues that it shows a partial accommodation towards the scientific model.

The final set of notions are characterised by the diagram (Fig 1.1) which Nussbaum & Novak provide.

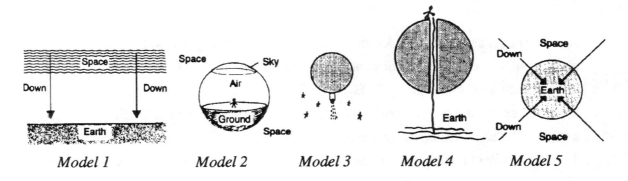

Model 1 *Model 2* *Model 3* *Model 4* *Model 5*

Fig 1.1: Diagram illustrating children's notions of the Earth concept and their progression.

Nussbaum and Novak postulate that such a schema represents a framework of conceptual progression although Nussbaum (1979) is more tentative about this hypothesis. Thus their work was an important contribution to establishing a developmental interpretation which was assessable with relatively simple and effective instruments and has since become the basis for several replication studies, all of which have effectively confirmed their analysis (Mali & Howe, 1979; Sneider & Pulos, 1983) and in addition, attempted further exploration of children's understanding.

The extra dimension in the work of these researchers was to administer a set of Piagetian science reasoning tasks. The results from these tests showed that there were moderate correlations between performance on these tasks and attainment of higher notions of the Earth concept which were significant ($p < .01$). Thus these data support the argument that formal thinking may be a necessary, but not a sufficient condition for the development of scientific understanding. In contrast, Nussbaum and Novak argue that their results, which shows that some 8 year old children hold the scientific concept of the Earth, expose the weaknesses of a Piagetian-based developmental psychology which stresses age-dependent maturation of cognitive capabilities. They contend that to hold such a model would require abstract formal reasoning, which conflicts with the prediction of the stage model that virtually no children are capable of such tasks at this age.

Sneider and Pulos also explored the correlation between a wide set of other variables and found that the development of the Earth concept is correlated with the amount of schooling and access to other sources of information. This result simply supports the argument that the development of the scientific idea is dependent on a child being exposed sufficiently to such thinking. Otherwise, children will develop intuitive, commonsense rationale for astronomical phenomena.

Another novel aspect to Sneider and Pulos' replication study was to break down Nussbaum's model into two dimensions, a scale for classifying children's understanding of the shape of the Earth, and a scale for classifying their conceptions about the behaviour of gravitational forces on the surface of the Earth. From an analysis of data collected in structured interviews with 159 children from the age 10 to 13, they firstly confirmed that Nussbaum and Novak's schema was a good model of children's progression. Additionally, their methodology enabled them to show that there is a strong correlation between children's responses about the shape of the Earth and their responses about the behaviour of gravity, finding that the correct conception of the Earth's shape is the antecedent of understanding that objects fall towards the centre of the Earth rather than the obverse. Finally they confirmed that there was a strong age related trend in the development of the Earth concept but considerable variation within any specific age.

Their study also looked at the influence of a range of other variables measuring children's verbal reasoning, their spatial ability, field independence/dependence and their interest in geography and science. An analysis of these data showed that verbal ability was a highly significant predictor of attainment of the Earth concept at all levels. They conclude that children's ideas can be explained by characterising them in terms of a 'physico-cultural' concept where the acquisition of cultural concepts requires the relating of observable phenomena (e.g. that things drop down in the context of a flat horizon) with what the child is told about the world (e.g. that it is spherical and only looks flat because we see a very small part at a time) and argue that their data show that understanding of physico-cultural concepts is related to the development of the ability to use a spatial frame of reference and verbal reasoning.

Finally the model developed by Nussbaum & Novak was also confirmed by Baxter (1989) who asked children to draw the Earth, then to draw some people on it and then add some rain falling from the clouds. Typically many children's drawings showed horizontal clouds set against a context of a circular Earth with rain falling vertically to the bottom of the page.

The clear conclusion to be drawn from these studies is that this model is a reliable interpretation of a large body of data extracted by different methods. Secondly, the consistency of the data supports the view that it is a valid picture of the stages of development that children go through in acquiring the Earth concept. However, whether all children go through all stages or whether they make transitions across several stages is an open question which only a longitudinal study would answer.

Other Astronomical Concepts

The core of the research work has looked at the child's conception of the Earth and their explanations for day and night. Only a few authors have gone beyond these areas. For instance, Baxter (1989) also investigated children's understanding of the phases of the Moon and the seasons using a mixture of interviews and a questionnaire. He found that the overwhelming majority of children's explanations of the phases of the Moon were based on the idea that the Earth cast a shadow on the Moon and, interestingly, the number who gave the scientific explanation essentially remained invariant between the age of 9 and 16. One explanation for this result could be the lack of treatment of this topic in many standard syllabi.

However, this argument would not apply to the explanation of the seasons which does feature in most science and geography courses. Baxter's data showed that the overwhelming majority at age 9-10 ($\approx 74\%$)[4] explained the seasons in terms of the Sun moving nearer and further away. At age 15-16, 53% of children were still using such an explanation and further evidence of the poor understanding of the Copernican model comes from Durant, Evans & Thomas (1989) who found that only 63% of adults were able to state that the Earth goes around the Sun, and of these, only 34% of adults knew that the Earth took one year to orbit the Sun.

One possible explanation for the dominance of this view is a confusion generated by the idea that the Earth's axis is tilted. Some children may interpret the information that the Northern hemisphere is 'tilted towards' the Sun in summer as meaning it is nearer, and 'tilted away' in winter as the opposite. Technically such interpretation is correct and we are marginally closer because of the tilt. But the real reason lies in the change in the altitude of the Sun which is a consequence of the tilt. The result is that in winter the same amount of radiant energy is spread over a much larger area of land than in summer and hence, in winter, the land is much cooler. The development of this particular misconception might be avoided if greater emphasis was given to the elliptical nature of the Earth's orbit and the fact it is 2 million miles *further away* from the Sun in June.

One interesting task is reported in the research undertaken by Vosniadou & Brewer (1990) who asked children if they could identify the Earth and Sun in pictures of the solar system. Only a small percentage of infant children were capable of identifying the Earth but by top juniors around 75% of children[5] managed this task. Similarly only 25% of the American infant children could recognise the Sun from a picture as opposed to 88% of the upper junior children. However, no sample size is given for these data so it is difficult to place too much reliance on these results.

---

[4] Unfortunately, Baxter presents all his data in a set of bar charts where the data have to be inferred. Hence the accuracy of such figures is $\pm 2.5\%$ at best.

[5] Apart from the data reported for Greek children where only 20% of top juniors correctly identified the Earth.

The development of children's thinking

For very young children, Piaget argued that artificialism is an original tendency based on the idea that all things have makers who are purposive, as opposed to animism where things themselves are purposive. He saw children's responses as being based on mental predilections associated with images more than concepts, and that children initially see objects as made by makers who are purposive so that 'made for man' is transformed by the child into 'made by man' who uses such reasoning to ascribe causality to a whole range of phenomena e.g. day and night. This notion is the essence of artificialism which ascribes causality to human or divine agents. However, this is not a God or a deity as conceived by adults, but one in which the child sees the role of parent and deity as synonymous. Hence artificialism is a product of the filial sentiment. But this tendency weakens as the child acts on the world and begins to appreciate that only some acts are technically feasible and realises the limitations of their parents. As a consequence, the child's sense of their parents' deity diminishes and instead, the child seeks to explain things in terms of interactions between objects and a purposiveness which is inherent to the object itself - hence the rise of animistic thinking. However, such thinking is still based on a commonsense interpretation of phenomena and some authors (Nussbaum, 1976; Vosniadou, 1987, 1991) argue that the change required for the child to attain the scientific understanding is a revolutionary shift in the structure of their knowledge which is only possible by relinquishing their intuitive thinking. Since the latter is grounded in a well-established set of fundamental beliefs generated from everyday experience, such change is inevitably an extended process.

Vosniadou's interest in this domain is based on the contrast between the scientific view of the Earth, Sun and Moon and children's intuitive cosmology. She argues that the child's knowledge is based on certain experiential beliefs and that development of the adult concept requires radical change in the child's epistemology and ontology. Table 1.1 summarises the main aspects of her argument and is clearly supportive of her hypothesis.

The key to conceptual change is the development of an understanding that the Earth is spherical and that it is possible to live on such a body without falling off. 80% of children who held such a belief were capable of explaining the phenomenon of day/night, a result supported by the earlier work of Sneider & Pulos who found that children who had such a concept of the Earth, also successfully explained the direction in which objects would fall. One of her key arguments is that children's knowledge is not fragmented since 85% of children made consistent use of one model in responding to a range of questions. But the conflict that is generated between the strong experiential basis for children's intuitive beliefs and the culturally accepted information does not lead to conceptual change. Instead, it leads to a progression in their misconceptions, e.g. a hollow Earth with an internal flat plane on which people live, as children try to resolve the conflict between their perceptions and their experience.

Feature	Intuitive Understanding	Scientific Understanding
Size of Solar Objects	Earth is larger than the Sun and Moon which are larger than the stars	Stars are suns which are larger than the Earth which is larger than the Moon
Shape of Earth	Earth is flat	Earth is spherical
Movement of Earth	Earth is stationary	Earth rotates on its axis and moves around the Sun on an elliptical orbit
Solar System	Rotates around the Earth (geocentric)	Rotates around the Sun (heliocentric)
Day & Night	Sun moves rising and setting	Earth moves, Sun stays still
Gravity	There exists an absolute down which is at right angles to the plane of the Earth and sky	Towards the centre of the Earth

Table 1.2: The main features of an intuitive epistemology and the scientific view of the Earth and Sun.

Evidence to support this view comes from an analysis of the data obtained from Nussbaum & Sharoni-Dagan's (1983) study of an instructional sequence delivered to second grade children in Israel. Children were assessed by interview before and after the sequence to determine what level of understanding of the Earth concept they had using the framework proposed by Nussbaum & Novak (Fig 1.1). Fig 1.2 shows the number of children holding each conception and the extent to which their ideas developed. Thus 17 children held model 1 and as a result of the instructional sequence, 1 child progressed two stages, 7 children advanced one stage and the remainder made no improvement in their understanding.

These data show that the majority of shifts were by one step and secondly, that the understanding of just under 50% of the children did not change. Vosniadou argues that the range of misconceptions is a result of a synthetic process by the child as it attempts to resolve its intuitive knowledge with the culturally accepted beliefs. Thus the child who views the Earth as a globe, where people live on flat planes inside the sphere, is able to reconcile his or her intuitive experiences with the ideas to which he or she is culturally exposed. Only the generative use of the Earth concept to provide explanations of physical phenomena will finally lead to resolution and acceptance of the scientific view but this does not destroy the intuitive concept, the two simply coexist. Such an argument supports Claxton's (1985) thesis that children simply operate with three sets of concurrent theories - gut science or intuitive reasoning for actions such as crossing the road, lay or popular science for explaining such events as atmospheric warming and school science within the context of the school laboratory.

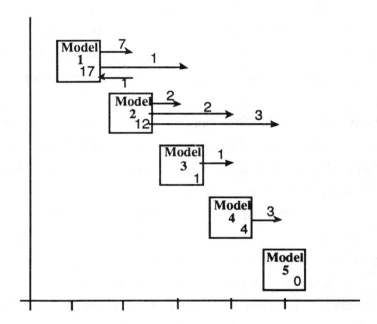

Fig 1.2: Diagram showing the levels of children's understanding of the Earth concept and the amount of shift as a result of Nussbaum & Sharoni-Dagan's teaching sequence. The figure in the bottom right hand corner of each box shows the number of children holding that model initially. The figures above the arrows show the numbers of children moving to a new model and the arrow shows the extent of their movement.

Surprisingly, the role of language in conceptual development is only considered, amongst the literature cited here, by Jones et al (1987) who point to its influence in the formation of children's early ideas e.g. 'the Sun grew tired and went to bed behind the hill' or simply that the statement 'the Sun rises/sets' implies intention on the part of the Sun. Thus everyday language simply reflects and reinforces children's animistic thinking and the commonsense observation that it is the Sun which moves across the sky and not the Earth which spins.

Pedagogic Approaches

Only the work of Nussbaum & Sharoni-Dagan examines the effect of an instructional sequence on children's understanding and whilst many of these researchers recognise the value of their work to a constructivist approach to teaching science, few elaborate how the approach outlined by Driver and Oldham (1985) can be applied. Vosniadou (1991) does make relevant points about instruction arguing that there is a need for lessons to provide experiences and opportunities for children to consider how it is possible for a round object to appear flat. Secondly, the knowledge that gravity acts toward the centre of the Earth is crucial to the establishment of the concept of a spherical Earth. Until this is understood, it is impossible for children to see how they can live on a spherical ball and not fall off. She proposes two possible mechanisms for instruction - Socratic dialogue and the use of analogies, metaphors and physical models though without any evidence to substantiate the validity of such a pedagogy.

The fundamental problem for all teachers in this domain is that the relevant knowledge e.g. that the Earth is a sphere and rotates is not accessible to direct perception and investigation. Only when children are able to relate explanations of imagined entities e.g. enormous suns or barren moons, to the descriptions of the perceived phenomena will they be able to change their understanding. Thus the development of an understanding in astronomy requires the ability to transcend the concrete and abstract from secondary sources. Baxter acknowledges this point in his statement that 'it is recognised that the construction of the heliocentric view involves a number of complex factors and it may not be appropriate to expect such an understanding before early adolescence'. When the latter factor is combined with Vosniadou's (1991) argument for the need to develop metacognitive awareness in children - that is to make them appreciate that their own ideas are naive theories, and the evidence for the limited effectiveness of instruction - it is apparent that conceptual development in this domain is a difficult and complex task for teachers.

If there are key concepts which have to be assimilated for a fundamental restructuring of ideas to occur, the pedagogic issue becomes one of how best to achieve such a process. For instance, Vosniadou & Brewer (1990) support general criticisms of Piagetian stage theory and argue that the changes observed can require a radical restructuring of domain specific knowledge, a thesis which was essentially proposed by Carey (1985) from her work on the development of children's biological knowledge. Thus any approach must aim to reformulate domain specific knowledge and the research reported here shared this perspective, being based on the general

THE LEARNING CENTRE 092125
EAST BERKSHIRE COLLEGE AT MAIDENHEAD

constructivist view that children's initial ideas are an important aspect of the process of assimilation and accommodation - important both to the teacher in assessing the initial level of the child's understanding, and important to the child who interprets new information using his or her existing framework of ideas. Only by providing opportunities for the teacher to elicit this information, and for the child to reflect on their own thinking and assimilate new ideas would there be any possibility of conceptual change.

References

Baxter, J. (1989) Children's Understanding of Familiar Astronomical Events. *International Journal of Science Education,* 11, 502-513.

Carey, S. (1985) *Conceptual Change in Childhood.* Cambridge, Mass: MIT Press.

Claxton, G. L., (1985) Teaching and Acquiring Scientific Knowledge in *Kelly in the Classroom: educational applications of Personal Construct Psychology.* Montreal: Cybersystems, Inc.

Driver, R. & Oldham, V. (1985). A Constructivist Approach to Curriculum Development. *Studies in Science Education,* 13, 105-122.

Durant, J. R., Evans, G. A. & Thomas, G. P. (1989) The Public Understanding of Science. *Nature,* 340, 11-14.

Finegold, M. & Pundak, D. (1991) A study of change in students' conceptual frameworks in astronomy. *Studies in Educational Evaluation,* Vol 17, 151-166.

Jones, L. B., Lynch, P. P. & Reesink, C.   (1987) Children's Conceptions of the Earth, Sun and Moon. *International Journal of Science Education,* 9, 1, 43-53.

Klein, C. (1982) Children's Concepts of the Earth and the Sun: A Cross-Cultural Study. *Science Education,* 65,1, 95-107.

Mali, G. & Howe, A. (1979) Development of the Earth and Gravity Concepts among Nepali Children. *Science Education,* 63,5, 685-691.

Nussbaum, J. & Novak, J. D. (1976) An Assessment of Children's Concepts of the Earth Utilizing Structured Interviews. *Science Education,* 60, 4, 535-550.

Nussbaum, J. & Sharoni-Dagan, N. (1983). Changes in Second Grade Children's Preconceptions About the Earth as a Cosmic Body Resulting from a Short Series of Audio-Tutorial Lessons. *Science Education,* 67, 1, 99-114.

Nussbaum, J. (1979) Children's Conceptions of the Earth as a Cosmic Body: A Cross Age Study. *Science Education,* 63,1, 83-93.

Piaget, J. (1929) *The Child's Conception of the World.* London: Routledge & Kegan Paul.

Sneider, C & Pulos, S. (1983) Children's Cosmographies: Understanding the Earth's Shape and Gravity. *Science Education*, 67, 2, 205-221.

Vosniadou, S. (1991) Conceptual Development in Astronomy in Glynn, S. M, Yeany, R. H. & Britton, B. K. (Eds) *The Psychology of Learning Science*. New Jersey: Lawrence Erlbaum.

Vosniadou, S. & Brewer, W. F. (1987) Theories of Knowledge Restructuring in Development. *Review of Educational Research,* 57,1,51-67.

Vosniadou, S & Brewer, W.F. (1990). A cross-cultural investigation of knowledge acquisition in astronomy: Greek and American data in Mandl, H., DeCorte E., Bennett N. & Friederich, H.C. (Eds), *Learning and Instruction: European research in an International context*. (Vol 3). Oxford: Pergamon.

2. Methodology

Sample

a. Schools

Ten schools from the London area were chosen for this research from three local authorities (Inner London, Newham and Barnet). One teacher from each school participated in the project. Most of the schools were selected by the research officer who had already been working in the locality providing support to primary schools in the development of primary science work in a previous post.

b. Teachers

Most of the teachers invited to participate in the project were known to the researchers from previous work in the SPACE project. This was advantageous in providing a pre-existing relationship and link between researcher and teachers which could be developed. Teachers were able to use this relationship to express their uncertainties about the work and ask for clarification. Unfortunately, the local authority was unable to release any of the teachers due to the difficulties experienced during this phase in obtaining any supply cover in the London area. This meant that all meetings had to take place during the teachers' own time after school, and this had the effect of curtailing the extent of the teacher contribution to the research on this topic.

The teacher's normal style of working varied, between individuals who made sole use of classrooms organised around groups using a topic approach and an 'integrated' day, and those who preferred to keep the class working together on a common theme. Teachers were encouraged to integrate the activities into their existing mode of working as there was a limit to the amount of change in teaching style that could be expected of them.

Many of the difficulties experienced and expressed by teachers with a topic were associated with a lack of confidence in their own understanding of the background science. In particular, this results in a concern about the level of understanding that it would be reasonable to expect a child to achieve. Whilst teachers understood that the research project was attempting to provide some insight into the latter question, it was clear that the degree of uncertainty was a source of anxiety for teachers. Teachers therefore found the regular contact with a researcher who had a scientific background valuable in providing support.

Names of the participating schools are provided in Appendix 1.

c. Children

Despite the limitation to a particular locale, the schools used reflect the wide variation seen in the London area between schools based in deprived areas and those with a substantial middle-class catchment area. Hence the children used in the sample represent those with a wide range of ability and ethnic background. All children in the classes of the participating teachers were used for the pre- and post-intervention elicitation activities. Inevitably there were some who were not present for both phases of the activity and the data collected from these children have not been used.

For the purpose of analysis, the children have been grouped by age into infants (5-7), lower juniors (8-9) and upper juniors (10-11). In case of any doubt surrounding the particular grouping of a child, the year of schooling was used to decide the appropriate cohort for a child. Data were generally obtained by individual interview though some of the data from lower and upper junior children, were obtained through written responses.

d. Liaison

During the data-collection phase of the project, the research was conducted by two people working part-time with the schools and the relevant teachers. Each member of the team was allocated particular schools. The researchers would meet on a regular basis to plan and co-ordinate the research, exchange information and develop materials.

The Research Programme

Classroom work on the topic of 'the Earth in Space' took place over a relatively long period in the school year which can be summarised as follows.

Pilot Exploration	Sept 90
Pre-Intervention Data Collection	Oct 90

Intervention	Nov 90
Post-Intervention Data Collection	Dec90 -Jan 91

The pilot exploration phase was based on interviews with a small number of children (20). These interviews used a wide range of questions to explore the nature of children's understanding of the processes of life and associated concepts. In addition, drawings and answers to written questions were employed to examine how valuable and reliable such sources were for eliciting children's meanings and understanding. The exploratory nature of this phase was required to supplement the small amount of literature there was available on the nature of young (5-11) children's understanding of this topic, and to explore how suitable the questions were for eliciting children's understanding of the concepts. Some of the questions devised for probing children's ideas were modifications of methods that had been used previously by other researchers. At the end of this phase, the data were examined to determine which were the most valuable lines of approach for eliciting children's ideas. The other valuable feature of this phase was that it provided time for developing a relationship with the teacher and the children so that they could become accustomed to the mode of working required.

Essentially, the classroom elicitation techniques were refined by the pilot process and the experience provided an opportunity for teachers and researchers to develop familiarity with the material and with each other. Data on children's ideas were then collected from children in classrooms using the selected activities. These questions and activities are shown in Appendix 2. The main methods of elicitation relied on a mixture of interviews, written answers and children's drawings. All the data from infant children were collected by interview and drawings as these children found it very difficult to provide written answers to questions.

The intervention activities were designed in consultation with the teachers and from an examination of the data collected previously. The data suggested several areas of interest for possible conceptual development and a framework of activities was designed which could be used by children to test their own ideas and explore their thinking in this domain. This was not presented as a prescriptive framework, but simply as a range of exercises and activities which could be used by children. Teachers and children were free to try other lines of investigation they wished to pursue. After the completion of the intervention phase, the same set of elicitations was used with the children as those used in the elicitation prior to the intervention.

Defining 'Earth in Space'

Any attempt to develop a child's concepts needs to be based on a definition of what a preferred understanding would be. In the earlier research, a list of concepts was compiled by the team to provide a map of ideas considered an *a priori* necessity for the development of the scientist's world view. However, in this instance, the National Curriculum Order had been published and the framework of the research changed. The Order defined, in a set of attainment targets, learning objectives for children to achieve in a progressive, developmental fashion. Whilst the Order and their articulation of the targets within it are open to debate, they represented at the time, the standard objectives that many teachers would be using for their teaching. Hence the decision was made to adopt these statements as guidelines of what it might be reasonable for a child to be expected to know. This does not imply that the team necessarily accepted these statements as reasonable expectations but they did constitute a set of aims for many teachers and their children. Therefore the research set out to ask whether they were reasonable expectations.

The National Curriculum was defined in terms of a set of attainment targets and programmes of study. The attainment targets (Table 2.1) represented assessment objectives on a 10 level scale. An able infant is expected to achieve level 3 by age 7 whilst an average child would achieve level 2. An able junior should achieve level 5 by the age 11 whilst an average child would achieve level 4. The programmes of study (Table 2.2) merely defined the set of experiences that should enable the attainment targets to be achieved.

The purpose of this list is to provide a framework or point of reference for the research where these statements represent a collection of ideas that children *may* develop by age 11. The principal difference between this research and earlier work on light and electricity, is that this is an externally defined list. One of the subsidiary aims of this research is to examine to what extent, as a consequence of the experiences that were provided by this research programme, such ideas develop in children and at what ages.

Level	Old Attainment Target[1]	New Attainment Target
1	Pupils should: • be able to describe through talking, or other appropriate means, the seasonal changes that occur in the weather and other living things. • know the danger of looking directly at the Sun. • be able to describe, in relation to their home or school, the apparent daily motion of the Sun across the sky.	Pupils should: • be able to describe the apparent motion of the Sun across the sky.
2	• be able to explain why night occurs. • know that day length changes throughout the year. • know that we live on a large, spherical, self-contained planet, called Earth. • know that the Earth, Moon and Sun are separate bodies.	• know that the Earth, Moon and Sun are separate spherical bodies
3	• know that the inclination of the Sun in the sky changes during the year. • be able to measure time with a sundial.	• know that the appearance of the Moon and the altitude of the Sun change in a regular and predictable manner
4	• know that the phases of the Moon change in a regular and predictable manner. • know that the Solar System is made up of the Sun and planets, and have an idea of its scale. • understand that the Sun is a star.	• be able to explain day and night, day length and year length in terms of the movement of the Earth around the Sun
5	• be able to relate a simple model of the solar system to day/night and year length, changes of day length, seasonal changes and changes in the inclination of the Sun. • be able to observe and record the shape and surface shading of the phases of the Moon over a period of time.	• be able to describe the motion of the planets in the solar system

Table 2.1: Attainment Target 1-5 of the English & Welsh National Curriculum (DES, 1989) and (DES, 1991)[1] for the Earth in Space component

---

[1] Since the publication of this Order, a revised publication has been produced by the Department for Education in 1991. The work reported here was based on the original Order. The summary and conclusions of this work are based on the new order (DES, 1991)

The programmes of study were as follows.

Key Stage 1[1]	Children should observe closely their local natural environment to detect seasonal changes, including day-length, weather and changes in plants and animals, and relate these changes to the passage of time. They should observe, over a period of time, the length of the day, the position of the Sun, and where possible the Moon, in the sky. They should investigate the use of a sundial as a means of observing the passage of time[2].
Key Stage 2	Children should be given the opportunity to investigate changes in the night sky, in particular the position of the Moon, through direct observation and by using secondary sources. Children should use a simple model of the solar system to attempt explanations of day and night, year length and changes in the aspect of the Moon and the elevation of the Sun. They should be introduced to the principle of the sundial as a means of noting the passage of time. They should learn about the position and motion of the Earth, Moon and Sun relative to each other[3].

Table 2.2: Programmes of Study for the English & Welsh National Curriculum in Science at Key Stage 1 & 2.

These ideas also provide a framework for examining children's ideas allowing three questions to be addressed.

a)   How different were the conceptions held by many children from such a framework and how disparate were their ideas?

b)   What development was observable in children's ideas across the age range?

c)   What potential did the planned intervention have for the development of children's ideas towards the scientist's view?

---

[1]   The term key stage refers to the period of education. Key Stage 1 is from age 5-7 (two years) and Key Stage 2 is from age 7-11 (four years).

[2]   In the 1991 order, this last sentence has been omitted from the programme of study for KS1 and added to the KS2 programme of study. There are other minor changes to the wording.

[3]   The only significant difference between this version of the order (1989) and the 1991 version is the addition of the sentence 'They should be introduced to the order and general movements of the planets around the Sun'.

This list was also used as a reference point for the development of the intervention. Given such a framework of objectives, the intervention task was to develop activities which would assist the formation of a fuller understanding of this domain by children. The activities were devised using simple materials familiar to children. Their primary role was to provide a focus for discussion of children's thinking and to challenge their existing ideas. Other considerations in designing activities were that the materials should be simple, easy to manipulate and safe to handle.

3. Children's Ideas about the Earth and Space

This chapter presents a qualitative picture of young children's thinking about the Earth and Space as found during the elicitation phases with individual or small groups of children. The work presented here draws from a carefully selected representative sample of children's drawings, writings and comments during interviews and uses summary charts to show general trends and give an overview of the main aspects of children's thinking in this domain. As such it does not claim to be comprehensive but simply presents a broad sketch of the typical thinking found in many children. The elicitation of their thinking was carried out by teachers and researchers using a subset of the activities employed during the pilot phase. The picture presented is based on a sample of 106 children (36 infants, 31 lower juniors and 39 upper juniors). Details of the elicitation activities are provided in Appendix 2.

The elicitation consisted of a mix of activities. Some responses required the children to write their answers; some required them to draw or add to drawings to show what they thought would happen, whilst some activities required the children to use simple materials as models and explain the reasoning for their choices and actions in individual interviews. In the case of infant children, all the responses were collected by individual interview because of the difficulty such children have in providing written responses.

The elicitation was designed to explore broadly seven areas of children's understanding and knowledge. These were:

1. What understanding of time did children have?
   Appendix 2, Section A, Question 1 & 2

2. What did children know about the movement of the Sun through the year?
   Appendix 2, Section B, Question 1, 2 & Section D, Question 1

3. What explanations did children give for the phenomena of day and night?
   Appendix 2, Section A, Question 3 & Section D, Question 1

4. What did children know about the daily movement of the sun and related phenomena?
   Appendix 2, Section A, Question 2 & Section B, Question 3 & 4.

5. What concept of the Earth did children have?
   Appendix 2, Section C, Question 1, 2 & 3 & Section D, Question 1

6. What was children's knowledge of distance?
   Appendix 2, Section D, Question 4 & 5

7. What knowledge of astronomical bodies did children have?
   Appendix 2, Section C, Question 3 & 4.

The results obtained are discussed under these general headings and a full analysis of the data can be found in Chapter 5. Data presented here are only from the elicitation prior to the intervention as the intention of this chapter is to provide an overview of children's thinking at that stage. Further information about these data, their interrelationships and the effects of the intervention can be found in chapter 5.

What understanding of time did children have?

Explanations of day and night, the changes in the seasons or the movement of the stars will have little meaning if a child has not assimilated and understood the concept of time and the meaning of terms such as year, month, week, day, hour and their interrelationships. Whilst very young children can clearly divide the day into 'day' and 'night', the appreciation that there is a consistent regularity to the daily changes which are measured and defined by hours is the basis for recognising that there is a phenomenon in need of explanation. Why, for instance, does the Sun always rise in the morning, reach its highest at midday and go down in the evening?

A similar argument can be made for the significance of understanding ideas such as the week, month and year. The former two are the subunits which are the foundations of the concept of year. If these are not understood it is unlikely that any child has internalised such an idea.

After some trialling it was found that the simplest method of exploring children's knowledge of these concepts was to use direct questions which asked how long is a day, month and year. The chart in Fig 3.1 shows a summary of children's responses.

What these charts show clearly is the evident progression and assimilation by children of all ages of three ideas with a rapid improvement whilst the children are in their lower junior years.

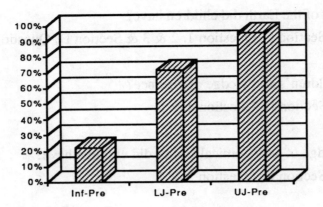

Fig 3.1: Chart showing percentage of children correctly answering the question 'How long is a day?'.

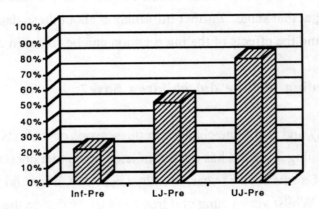

Fig 3.2: Chart showing percentage of children correctly answering the question 'How long is a month?'.

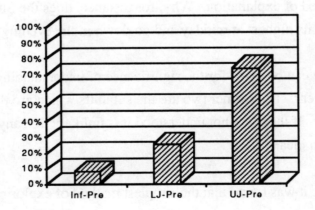

Fig 3.3: Chart showing percentage of children correctly answering the question 'How long is a year?'.

Further analysis of the data (Chapter 5) showed that there was a strong interdependence between children who were successful on one item and another which suggests that the general concept of time has a unitary or holistic aspect for most children. The implication is that infant children might find understanding such ideas difficult and hence it would be unproductive for infant teachers to devote much effort to this topic.

What did children know about the movement of the Sun through the year?

Several questions were used here to establish if children were aware of seasonal differences and then to see what model they used to explain such variation. It was expected that if children were not aware of these differences it would be unlikely that they had assimilated any idea which would explain variations between the seasons.

The first question simply asked children to think of three differences between a summer and a winter day. Naturally the overwhelming response that most children gave was that it was hotter in summer. At all ages more than 50% gave this response and typical answers were:

'It's windy in winter and cold. In summer it's hot and sunny.'

Mahfogur: Age 10

'Summer is hotter than winter.'

Jaffrey: Age 10

'Summer is different from winter because its colder in winter. Sometimes it snows and there's fog

Zeeshan: Age 8

However, there were a small minority who mentioned other attributes of seasonal differences.

'There is different weather, different lightness and it's different in dark. The time changes in winter. At 4 o'clock it's dark.'

Naheen: Age 10

'A summer day is hot. There are flowers. There is no snow.

Venetia: Age 11

'In winter the days are much shorter.' Zarina: Age 11

'In winter the sun is quite down.'

Haroon: Age 7

'In summer we play outside, in winter we stay at home.' Zilani: Age 6

In the second question exploring their understanding of this area, children were asked to add to the following drawing to show the position of the Sun, firstly at midday in winter and then, at midday in summer. Fig 3.4 shows the predominant response showing the position of the Sun in both seasons at the same level given by all groups (infants 92%, lower juniors 48% and upper juniors 79%).

Fig 3.4: Typical response given by children to question asking to draw the position of the Sun in the middle of the day in the summer (S) and in winter (W)

The percentage giving the correct response was 8%, 29% and 8% respectively (infants, lower juniors, upper juniors) and after the intervention, this had only increased to 14%, 32% and 23%. These data show that very few children were aware of the difference in altitude of the Sun above the horizon between summer and winter. Since this observation and knowledge is an a priori necessity for the formulation of an explanation of the phenomenon, it is to be expected that only very few children would be able to offer a correct description. A common error in their responses was to show correctly the distinction as a difference in the vertical displacement but, with the Sun in winter shown as being higher than that in summer (Fig 3.5).

Whilst it is not self-evident what it is that makes this particular observation so difficult to assimilate, there was some evidence that the effect of the intervention was to increase the numbers of children who showed the distinction between summer and winter as being one in the vertical direction.

Fig 3.5: Response showing a vertical, but erroneous difference in position
of the summer and winter Sun.

The other peculiar feature of the data is that there was no progression in children's
understanding. The group that was most successful in responding to this item was the
lower junior group whilst the upper juniors had more difficulty in correctly answering
this question. This result was abnormal in that the general trend for most items was for
facility to increase with age.

Their understanding of the seasons was explored further by asking children to model
the movements of the Sun and Earth through the year. They were asked to choose
from a selection of objects of different shape (spheres, discs, cylinders and rectangles
of 2 different sizes) and show how they thought they moved. The interviewer assisted
by offering to hold one of the shapes and move it as instructed. The broad features of
children's responses are shown in Table 3.1. Clearly for a large number of children
this task was too difficult and it is only a majority of upper junior children who were
able to provide a meaningful response.

	Inf-Pre	LJ-Pre	UJ-Pre
One body moves	41%	29%	69%
Both bodies move	3%	5%	3%
No response	56%	64%	28%

Table 3.1: Percentage of children in each group giving a response that showed one body moving, both bodies moving or no response. (Percentages have been rounded)

Of those that did manage to demonstrate a model successfully, the majority showed only one body moving, though this was not always the Earth.

Fig 3.6 shows the percentages of these children who indicated that it was the Earth that moved around the Sun. This idea had only been adopted by a majority of upper juniors. However, this result can be viewed as quite promising as it shows that the Copernican view of the Earth, which does not place the Earth at the centre of the Universe, has already been grasped by large numbers of children by the age of 10/11. Given the historical difficulty that such an idea encountered, it is encouraging to see that it no longer causes quite the same problem.

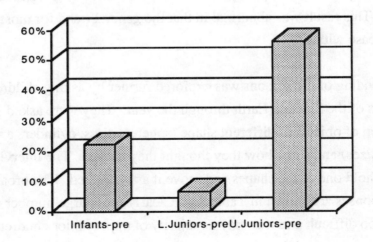

Fig 3.6: Percentage of children giving the Copernican response that it is the Earth which moves around the Sun.

Children who did not know the answer to this question tended to give no response and gave the impression of being genuinely perplexed as if the question was something which they had never considered. Of those that did give a response which was not the scientific idea, many offered the view that the Sun was going around the Earth or that the Sun moved away from the Earth during Winter whilst the Earth remained static. Finally, it is interesting to note that the data show some evidence for a U-shaped progression in children's understanding of this concept - that is the number having the Copernican world view diminishes in the lower juniors and then climbs significantly in the upper juniors.

What explanations did children give for the phenomena of day and night?

The phenomenon of day and night is self-evidently part of every child's experience. Hence it is interesting to see if children are capable of theorising and attempting to provide an explanation of nightfall and the apparent disappearance of the Sun, and whether their explanations are based in physical phenomena. Two questions were asked of children. Firstly 'What happens to the Sun at night?' which was followed by the question 'Can you tell me why night happens?'.

The answer to the first question produced a range of responses of which the following are typical and reflect similar responses found by Piaget.

'It goes away.'   Victoria: Age 7

'The Earth turns round and it blocks the Sun's way so that it is dark.'
                                                                       Nazia: Age 8

'The Sun goes down and the moon comes up.'   Romana: Age 9

'It stays down behind the mountains.'   Haroon: Age 7

'It changes into a moon.'   Aaron: Age 9

'It is hidden by other planets and our moon.'   Venetia: Age 10

Older children tended to produce the scientific response or a version of it. However some of these responses display a geocentric view of astronomical movements.

'Goes to America, then goes round the world.' John: Age 11
'It goes to the other side of the Earth.' Yazdan: Age 10

'We cannot see it cos we turn away from it.' Kelly: Age 10

'Because the earth moves, the earth faces away from the Sun.' Naheen: Age 11

Fig 3.7 shows the main categories of response and their frequency for each age group. More than half the infants and lower juniors simply provided a descriptive response that the Sun goes down which would imply that these children showed no need to provide any explanation of the advent of night. The other statements all rely on a causal mechanism which would indicate some ability to theorize on the part of these children.

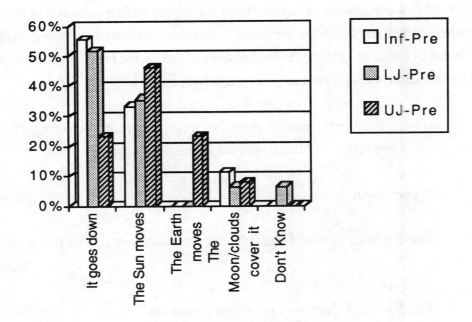

Fig 3.7: Chart showing the range of explanations offered by children for the phenomenon of night and the percentages offering each type.

However, the predominant response was that the Sun moves and shows that the majority of children who did provide a causal mechanism believed in the notion of a geocentric solar system with the Sun orbiting the Earth. Only amongst the upper juniors did several (21%) offer the explanation that it is the Earth that moves and this result indicates that the scientific idea is probably difficult for children to understand and accept. That the scientific explanation is not understood is hardly surprising, as the evidence of commonsense reasoning is that it is the Sun that moves and there is no direct observations to the contrary. Traditional scientific explanations rely on appeals to experiences of relative motion in trains at stations where it easy to be confused as to which train is moving, or alternatively, photographs of the stars taken at night over long exposures. The circular trails produced would require all the stars to be rotating around one central star if the Earth is static and it is normal to argue that such a state of affairs is highly unlikely. The hypothesis that it is the Earth that moves is a much simpler explanation and therefore preferred. However in a later question (see beneath), requiring children to use shapes to provide an explanation, many more children (infants - 21%, lower juniors - 41%, upper juniors - 52%) showed that night happens because the Earth rotates on its axis which casts doubt on the validity of this result. The difference in response between these two questions suggests that the use of models may have been a more effective method for eliciting children's knowledge of the explanation for the physical phenomena.

The second question asked children more directly for an explanation of the reason for night occurring if it had not already been proffered. The percentages who provided a physical response show a steady increase across the age range. What was interesting about the responses to this question was the large number of children (infants 68%, lower juniors 42%, upper juniors 38%) who gave a personal reason for night. Typical responses were:

'People have to have a rest.'	*Haroon: Age 8*
'Cause if we didn't we won't be able to get any rest.'	*Rizwan: Age 8*
'We want to sleep.'	*Victoria: Age 7*

The large number of such responses supports the view that the child's perception of the world is highly egocentric. Events happen to meet the needs of the child hence night happens because people need to sleep. An alternative hypothesis is that such responses show such children equate 'night' with 'the time you go to sleep' rather than the onset of darkness and that such children are operating with an alternative conception. The data do show that such responses diminish with older children, indicating that such thinking declines with age.

The final question to explore this aspect of their understanding was one where children where asked to pick two objects from a range of shapes (sphere, discs, semi-circular discs, semi-spheres and rectangles), one to represent the Earth and one to represent the Sun, and then use these to show how they moved in one day and night. This question aimed to explore if children were capable of modelling what happens, and if any models that they used represented the standard scientific explanation.

Fig 3.8 shows two aspects of their responses - the percentage who were incapable of providing any response at all and hence found the process of modelling the event beyond them, and the percentage who correctly indicated that it was the Earth that moves rather than the Sun.

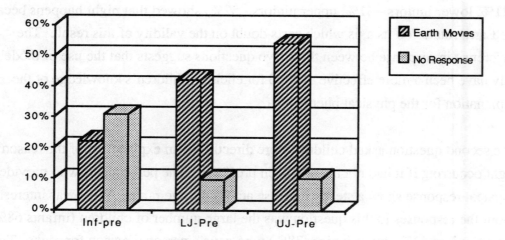

Fig 3.8: Percentage of children who a) gave no response and b) indicated that it was the Earth that moved when asked to use shapes to show how these object moved during one day and night.

The obvious feature of these results is that the difficulty of the task declined with age. In all cases a majority of the children attempted to use the shapes to model what happened and this would imply that the idea of using representational objects to explain a physical phenomenon is accepted by children at this age. The other aspect was that many more children indicated that it is the Earth that moves than in the earlier question. Thus this method is possibly a more effective means of eliciting children's knowledge of what happens as it is not possible to give descriptive answers of the kind 'the Sun goes down'. If so then this result shows that more than half the upper junior children have appreciated the scientific explanation and can repeat it. In itself, it is quite remarkable that so many children have achieved this understanding by this age as the intuitive commonsense explanation is that it is the Sun that moves and not the Earth. The intervention was also successful in increasing the understanding of this idea as correct responses were provided by 74% of lower juniors and 82% of upper juniors in the post-elicitation.

What did children know about the daily movement of the Sun and related phenomena?

The daily movement of the Sun is one of the simplest phenomena which children will observe from a very early age. The question of interest in this research was whether children knew the daily path followed by the Sun through the sky, for without a model of the movement of the Sun, children would lack one of the requisite pieces of knowledge to explain the variation in shadow length and direction during the course of a day. Therefore several questions were used to explore whether children had such knowledge of the daily movement.

The first question showed an urban scene looking South and children were asked to add to the picture to show the position of the Sun a) in the early morning, b) in the middle of the day and c) in the afternoon. The urban scene was chosen in preference to a blank horizon as the latter was judged to be unfamiliar to the children who were the subject of this research. A response that was judged to be correct is shown in Fig 3.9. This shows the correct sequence, with the Sun rising in the East and setting in the West, with the midday Sun shown at a higher elevation above the horizon than either the morning or afternoon Sun.

Fig 3.9: Correct response to question asking children to show the position of the Sun during the morning, midday and afternoon.

However, this type of response, showing the correct sequence and the correct relative height at midday, was only provided by 6% of infants, 20% of lower juniors and 10% of upper juniors. The low facility on this item was somewhat surprising given that this is a simple observation which children of these ages would have had plenty of opportunity to make. A large proportion of the responses showed the Sun moving in the correct direction, from East to West, but without any variation in the altitude of the Sun above the horizon. A typical response is shown in Fig 3.10.

Fig 3.10: Typical incorrect response to question asking children to show the position of the Sun during the morning, midday and afternoon.

A significant percentage of the children (11% of infants, 19% of lower juniors and 26% of upper juniors) showed the sequence of the daily movement of the Sun in the reverse order from West to East as shown in Fig 3.11.

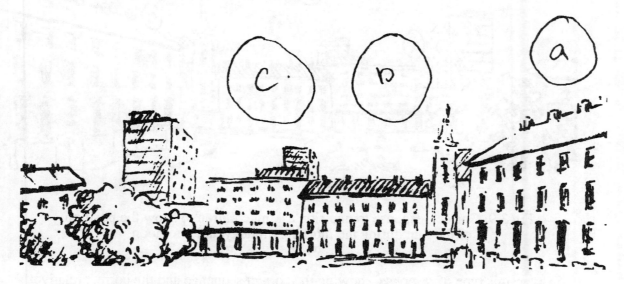

Fig 3.11: Response to question asking children to show the position of the Sun during the morning, midday and afternoon showing Sun moving from West to East.

The third type of error (Fig 3.12) was simply to show the three positions of the Sun in a vertical sequence though this was only done by small minorities of infants (6%), no lower juniors (0%) and upper juniors (23%).

Fig 3.12: Response to question asking children to show the position of the Sun during the morning, midday and afternoon showing Sun placed in a vertical sequence.

Why children found this item difficult is unclear. Possibly the drawing showing an urban environment was difficult for them to interpret and the errors are those associated with a lack of perspective and drawing skills rather than any lack of knowledge. It is also possible that living in such an environment makes it difficult to note the regular repetition of the Sun's movement across the horizon. It would have been interesting to repeat the item with a rural scene and a horizontal horizon and any teachers using this item for their own investigations are definitely recommended to use such a drawing as well.

That many more children do know about the daily trajectory of the Sun is shown by their responses to the next question which explored if children were aware of the daily movement of shadows produced by a stick. Such knowledge is essential to understand how a sundial works. In this question, children were asked to add to a drawing, showing a tree, the Sun and the shadow of the tree early in the morning, to show the position of the shadow at midday. There are essentially two features of interest in their response - did they show the shadow shorter and attached correctly to the tree, and was the position of the shadow correctly shown i.e. towards the bottom of the paper ? Any child who gave such a response had a well-formed understanding of the daily movement of the Sun and the relationship between shadow length and the altitude of the Sun.

There was a wide range of responses to this question. At the lowest level, over and above no response at all, children simply added shapes to the drawing which were detached from the tree, bore no similarity to its shape and no relationship to the position of the Sun. Fig 3.13 shows a slightly better response of an infant child who sees no relationship between shadow, tree and Sun other than a vague attempt to draw something which has an equivalent shape.

Fig 3.13: Response to question asking child (age 6) to show the position of the Sun at midday.

Another common error was to show the shadow in the correct position but no shorter or vice versa, a shorter shadow but in the wrong position. Fig 3.14(a) and Fig 3.14(b) show examples of both such responses.

The number of children who responded to this question with the correct scientific interpretation showing the shadow shorter and towards the north was 19% of infants, 19% of lower juniors and 51% of upper juniors. The much higher success rate on this question contrasts notably with that on the previous one, particularly since this question makes more substantive cognitive demands on a child. For, to provide the correct response, he or she would have had to know that the midday sun has a higher altitude and been able to argue in terms of a compensation, i.e. as the Sun gets higher, the shadow goes shorter and as the Sun goes one way, the shadow goes the other way. Then, these two pieces of reasoning have to be combined to produce the correct answer. Thus the question raised by this item is whether the child has access to the necessary powers of cognitive reasoning to correctly answer such a question.

Fig 3.14(a) Response to question asking child (age 9) to show the position of the shadow at midday.

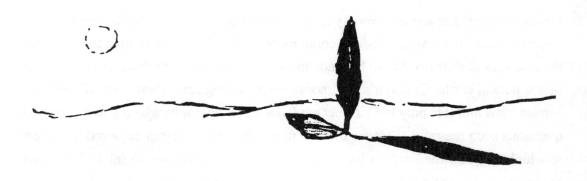

Fig 3.14(b) Response to question asking child (age 9) to show the position of the shadow at midday showing shortened shadow in the wrong position.

The final question in this area explored children's understanding in a more open-ended manner by asking them to explain how shadows could be used to tell the time. Responses elicited from children generally fell into three categories:

(i)   Those that showed the children had some understanding of the process and were considered to be generally valid in broad terms of which the following is an example:

*'When it is morning, the shadow will face to the right. When it is midday it
will be in between. When it is in the afternoon it will be on the left.'*

Yazdan: Age 10.

(ii)   Those that simply stated that it could be done with a sundial i.e.

'by a sundial'   *Scott: Age 10.*

(iii)   Finally, those who gave no response or stated that they did not know. This
category of no response was given by the majority (58% of infants, 52% of
lower juniors and 62% of upper juniors).

The percentage giving a generally valid response i.e. category (i) was very small - 14%
of infants, 16% of lower juniors and 10% of upper juniors which would suggest that
the sundial is not a simple topic which will be easily understood.

What concept of the Earth did children have?

Lewis Wolpert[1] has argued strongly that science is unnatural and that it requires 'un-
commonsense' reasoning. No idea could more typify his argument than the nature of
the ontological shift that has to be made in moving from a flat-earth conception to that
of a spherical earth. Children's commonsense reasoning leads them naturally to the
former view and it is only the indirect evidence of photographs which undermines and
questions such reasoning. Hence the first question in the research explored the extent
to which they saw the Earth as flat or spherical by asking children to select from a set of
shapes consisting of a sphere, a disc, a semi-circular disc, a semi-sphere and a
rectangle the shape which was most like Earth. No child chose either the semi-sphere
or the semi-circular disc and the percentage of children choosing each of the other
shapes is shown in Fig 3.15.

At first sight, these data would imply that the majority of children had accepted the
round-earth view unproblematically. However, further exploration of this concept was
undertaken using a modified item first used by Nussbaum and Novak[2]. This question

1   Wolpert, L. (1992) *The Unnatural Nature of Science.* London, Faber & Faber.
2   Nussbaum, J. (1979) Children's Conceptions of the Earth as a Cosmic Body: A Cross Age
Study, *Science Education*, 63, (1), 83-93.

shows children a drawing of a sphere which represents the Earth with diagrammatic people shown on the top, on the side and towards the 'bottom' holding a ball in their hand. Children are asked to add to the drawing to show what happens to the ball when it is released. This item was modified by adding the continents to the sphere to make it appear more realistic.

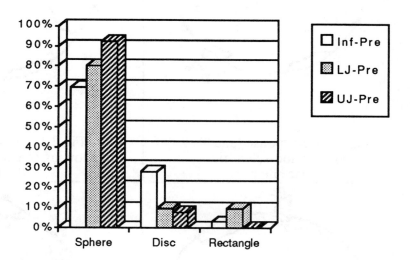

Fig 3.15: Chart showing the percentage of children choosing each type of shape. Children's responses fell into four categories: those that showed the balls falling vertically to the bottom of the page (Fig 3.16); those that showed the ball falling radially inwards (Fig 3.17 and Fig 3.18); those that showed it moving radially outwards or a broad range of other responses e.g. the ball shown moving sideways across the surface of the Earth (Fig 3.19).

The essential argument for the analysis of children's responses is that those who are still clinging to the notion of a flat earth consisting of two horizontal planes, formed by the plane of the ground and the plane of the sky, have developed a commonsense notion of 'down' which is at right angles to these two planes. In this problem, these two planes are formed by the top and bottom of the page and children with this idea will show the balls falling 'down' towards the bottom of the page.

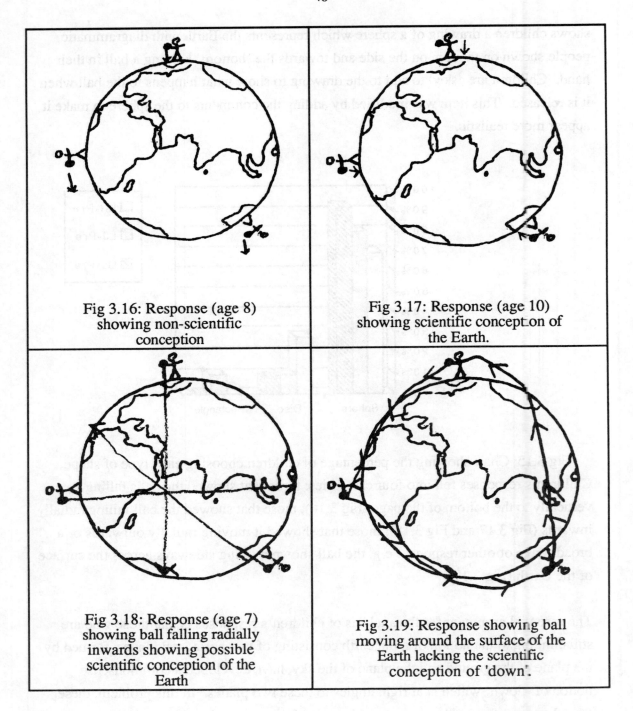

Fig 3.16: Response (age 8) showing non-scientific conception

Fig 3.17: Response (age 10) showing scientific conception of the Earth.

Fig 3.18: Response (age 7) showing ball falling radially inwards showing possible scientific conception of the Earth

Fig 3.19: Response showing ball moving around the surface of the Earth lacking the scientific conception of 'down'.

The scientific conception of 'down' towards the centre of the Earth is difficult to accept because children are naturally egocentric and view physical phenomena from their own perspective. To understand that people in Australia do not fall off requires a mental transformation which enables the child to see the world from other people's view.

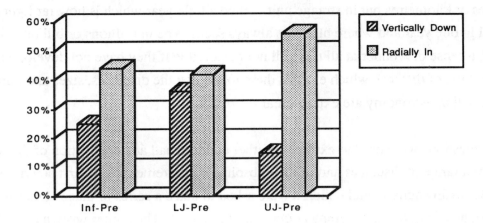

Fig 3.20: Chart showing percentage of children who marked the ball as falling towards the bottom of the page and those who showed it falling towards the centre of the Earth.

Fig 3.20 shows the data for the two types of responses shown in Fig 3.16 and Fig 3.17. For all ages there were a larger proportion showing the balls falling radially in compared to those showing it falling towards the bottom of the page. This result is surprising in the light of previous research by Nussbaum & Novak which indicated that a maximum of 22% of year 6 children had attained some aspects of the scientific conception of the Earth. There are two possible explanations for the difference between this research and theirs: firstly the drawing clearly shows that it is a representation of a globe whereas Nussbaum & Novak's was a simple unmarked sphere and secondly, Nussbaum & Novak used additional items which may have tested children's understanding more exhaustively. What both this result and that of Nussbaum & Novak's show, is that this idea is not as simple as it seems and requires the development of the child's ability to see objects from another's perspective. And, whilst the child's concept of a flat earth is reinforced daily, the only observational evidence to challenge this idea is the limited horizon of view from the top of a hill or tall building which is rarely available to urban children.

What is children's knowledge of distance?

Astronomy essentially deals with very large objects and very large distances. It makes demands on the human imagination asking that we envisage a world in which we are only the most microscopic component. Sir James Jeans put this into context aptly when he said that there are as many stars in the Universe as there are grains of sand on all the beaches in the world. It introduces a world where distances are measured not in metres or kilometres but in strange units called a light year which is how far light can travel in one year and where numbers always seem to be in millions or billions. For the child, a sense of wonder at all this will not be possible if they have not developed a conception of distance which enables them to see that the distances, sizes and numbers discussed in astronomy are extraordinary.

Two questions were used to explore whether children had any conception of the relative size of a range of distances and of their absolute measurement. The first activity was a simple sorting activity and children were asked to place a series of place names in order of distance from London commencing with the largest. The names written on the cards were the Sun, New York, Moon, Mars, Liverpool and Southend[3]. This task was not tried on infant children as the pilot trial had shown that the task had little or no meaning for them. For the lower juniors and upper juniors, 52% and 67% respectively were able to put them into the correct order with at most one item misplaced in the sequence. At first sight, these data imply that many of these children had assimilated a scale of distance which enabled them to successfully differentiate a wide variety of distances. However, when asked to give an absolute estimate of the scale of distance, they were much less successful. Responses were categorised as approximately correct if they were within ± 100% of the correct figure. Fig 3.21 shows the data for their responses and reveals that very few children had any conception of the real distance to this range of objects.

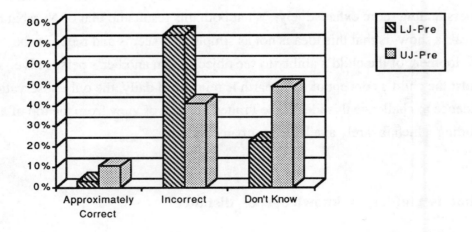

Fig 3.21: Chart showing percentage of children providing each category of response to question asking for an estimate of absolute distances to six objects.

---

3   For overseas readers, Liverpool is about 300 km from London and Southend is about 60 km from London.

That this is so should not be surprising. The ability to estimate distances is undoubtedly a sophisticated skill which is dependent on a wide range of experiential knowledge. Children of age 10/11 have had little experience of travel, cycling or walking which would help them to establish such a sense. However, it does imply that many children will find it difficult to appreciate the scale of the objects and the distances that separate them. Hence model making activities, where circles are constructed corresponding to the relative size of the planets or playground activities where children are used to represent the planets and their separation to scale, are both valuable activities in helping to provide concrete instances of the relative sizes and positions of the planet.

Finally, children were asked to do a second sorting activity which required them to sort six cards with the names the Sun, Moon, Earth, Jupiter, Mars, Saturn written on them by the size of the object indicated. The intention behind this was to explore whether children had any idea of the relative sizes of the objects in the Solar system. This task did prove to be more difficult but it is interesting to note that a third of upper juniors were capable of successfully answering this task. Given that performing the operation does require detailed knowledge of the bodies concerned, these data (Table 3.2) show that many children had already assimilated such knowledge.

	LJ-Pre %	UJ-Pre %
All Correct	0	33
All but one in the correct order	6	3
Sun, Earth & Moon in correct order only	23	3
Incorrect	71	62

Table 3.2: Percentage of children achieving each category of success on task to sort planets by size.

Further data on this aspect of children's knowledge were obtained by asking children to imagine that they were in a spacecraft and that there was a window through which they could see the Earth, Sun and Moon. The children were asked to draw what they might see. Three typical responses are shown in Fig 3.22, Fig 3.23 and Fig 3.24.

Fig 3.22: Child's (age 6) response to question asking for a drawing of the
Sun, Moon and Earth as seen from a spaceship window.

This drawing shows no differentiation between the sizes of the objects which contrasts
with the response shown in Fig 3.23 where the child does show some understanding of
the relative sizes; Fig 3.24 shows an example where the relative sizes are approximately
correct.

Fig 3.23: Child's drawing (age 9) showing Earth, Sun and Moon as seen
from window of a spaceship with the Earth largest.

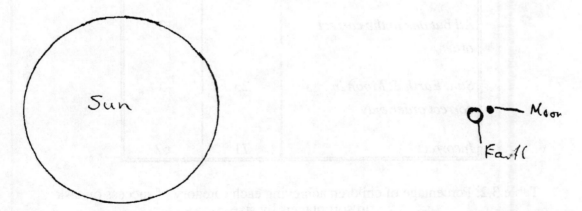

Fig 3.24: Child's (age 10) response to question asking for a drawing of the
Sun, Moon and Earth as seen from a spaceship window.

Fig 3.25 shows the distribution of the responses in percentage terms. Broadly the
number showing the three objects as being equal in size diminishes and the number

who are aware that the Sun is the largest increases. This pattern matches with previous data for the sorting activities which showed improved facility for older children. These data suggest that children's astronomical knowledge of objects and their sizes does improve with age.

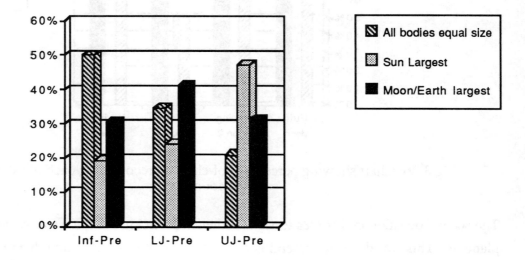

Fig 3.25: Chart showing the main features of children's drawings and the percentage of each group providing such responses.

What knowledge of astronomical bodies did children have?

A few questions were included to elicit the astronomical knowledge held by these children. The first question (Question 5, section B), explored whether children had any knowledge of the phases of the Moon. Five drawings of the Moon including a full moon, waxing and waning moon (2), and a half moon were shown and the child asked to mark which ones they had seen before. More than 80% of all children indicated that they had seen a full moon and more than 50% a waxing or waning Moon. The data (Fig 3.26) also show that there is little variation with age. The phase of the Moon that was least familiar to all groups was a half moon. In itself, the acquisition of such knowledge is of no great significance but since the national curriculum does suggest that children should undertake observations of the Moon, it does indicate that the observations will not be totally unfamiliar.

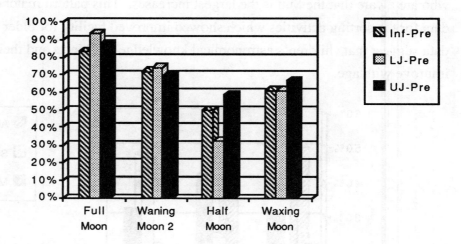

Fig 3.26: Chart showing percentage of children recognising each phase of the Moon.

The second question in this area tested whether children knew what a star is and what a planet is. This was done by presenting a list of eleven items and asking them to ring which they thought were stars (Section C, Question 4) and another list of 9 items and asking them to ring which they thought were planets. The data for the results for stars are shown in table 3.3 and for planets in table 3.4.

	Inf-Pre	LJ-Pre	UJ-Pre
Percentage giving correct response and marking only stars	6%	0%	13%
Sun and other items marked	8%	35%	31%

Table 3.3: Percentage of children giving the two responses that showed an understanding of the concept of a star.

These data show that very few children had any clear concept of what a star was. The figures for infants are more attributable to chance than any systematic understanding and it is only with the upper juniors that any significant understanding started to emerge. Children were more successful when they were asked to name a star. 0% of infants, 16% of lower juniors and 31% of upper juniors stated that the Sun was a star. The trend in the data is similar to that in table 3.3 though the facilities were different which may indicate that it is a mistake to attribute too much significance to the responses to any one item.

	Inf-Pre	LJ-Pre	UJ-Pre
Percentage giving correct response and marking only planets	3%	16%	33%
Some planets indicated	39%	29%	23%
All planets and some other items marked	36%	55%	41%
Incorrect	22%	0%	3%

Table 3.4: Percentage of children giving the three responses that showed an understanding of the concept of a planet.

The data in Table 3.4 show that many more children had at least some understanding of the concept of a planet since 97% of upper juniors gave a response that was at least partially correct. However a more reliable indicator would be the data obtained by adding the first two rows as it could be argued that the the third category of response really shows a failure to discriminate. Eliminating the third category of response still shows that more than 50% of upper juniors had a reasonable idea of what is meant by a planet as did 42% of infant children.

Further evidence of the nature and depth of their understanding comes from the shapes chosen by children to represent the Sun and Earth when modelling the explanation of day and night and the annual movement of the two objects. The percentage who picked two spheres with a larger one to represent the Sun was 28% of infants, 32% of lower juniors and 54% of upper juniors.

However their ability to use these to explain the origin of day and night and the annual movement of the Earth is much more limited as the data in table 3.5 show. This table shows the numbers who were able to give the two features of the scientific explanation for day and night that a) the Earth rotates and b) that it does so once every 24 hours. Secondly, it shows the percentage of those who were able to give both features of the Copernican explanation for the annual movement of the Earth around the Sun. Even in the upper juniors, less than one fifth were able to use the models to give the full explanation for day and night. Somewhat surprisingly, the more abstract Copernican explanation of the annual movement of the Sun was offered by a greater percentage of the upper juniors.

	Inf-Pre	LJ-Pre	UJ-Pre
Scientific Explanation of Day and Night	8%	3%	14%
Full Copernican explanation of the movement of Sun and Earth	8%	0%	44%

Table 3.5: Table showing the percentage of children who gave the full scientific explanation for day and night and the Copernican explanation for the annual movement of the Earth.

Summary

The picture of children's understanding that emerges from the data reported here briefly is one of a longitudinal progression in children's understanding of many aspects of astronomical knowledge with age. Thus their understanding of time progresses in what appears to be an almost linear fashion to the point where children of age 10/11 had a good understanding of the main subdivisions of the day and year.

Children's understanding of the yearly differences of both the position of the Sun and its daily movement was poor and only small minorities of even the upper juniors were able to show how the position of the Sun varies from Summer to Winter or how the Sun moved during the day. However in the latter case, a bare majority of upper juniors were able to show correctly the position of a shadow at midday which would suggest that they may have had a knowledge of the Sun's movement. This may be remediable through more explicit instruction which encourages children to record and observe the position of the Sun.

Data for their explanations for day and night are a little mixed in that questions simply eliciting a verbal response would indicate that the overwhelming majority of all ages hold the commonsense explanation that it is the Sun which moves. However, further exploration with the use of a range of shapes to model the Sun and Earth gave some indication that the geocentric explanation may be less widely held as the majority of upper juniors were able to show that the Earth spins.

Only one item was used to explore the child's concept of the Earth and whether they saw it as a cosmic body where individuals are attached by a gravitational force which acts towards the centre. The results are somewhat perplexing when contrasted with research reported elsewhere as they suggest that a significant minority of children of all ages hold the scientific view of the Earth. This suggests that further probes of children's understanding are required possibly to obtain a reliable view of their knowledge, possibly through the use of a question which shows an uncapped bottle, half-full at the South Pole and asks children what will happen to the water.

The data for children's understanding of distance suggest that the idea of a relative scale i.e which object is bigger than the next was established for the majority of children by the time they were age 8/9. However very few children had any real conception of the real distances and given their limited experience of travel, this is not surprising.

As for children's astronomical knowledge, the data show a mixed picture with a large majority of the children aware of a full Moon, a third of upper juniors knowing that the Sun was a star and large number of lower and upper juniors having some concept of a planet. This suggests that simple astronomical knowledge would appear to be in an emergent state.

4: The Intervention Phase

The previous chapter provides some insight into the range of ideas about the Earth in Space held by young children. Whilst this qualitative picture is valuable in providing an insight into children's astronomical knowledge and understanding, the aim of this research was to attempt to extend previous work by devising a set of intervention activities which could be used by teachers to develop children's thinking and astronomical knowledge.

The rationale that underpinned the design of the intervention was that the teaching and learning would begin with a phase in which children would be provided with an opportunity to articulate and explore their own thinking in this domain. This was done by providing children with a range of activities that elicited their thinking through drawing, writing and discussion. A qualitative review of much of the data has been presented in Chapter 3. The data obtained from the elicitation were used informally to provide the teachers with a familiarity and understanding of their children's thinking about the Earth in Space. A set of structured activities was then provided which would provide an opportunity for children to develop their understanding and knowledge.

This intervention was designed to use a range of activities which would provide an opportunity for children to represent and clarify their thinking in more detail. This was generally done through drawings or group discussion. The criterion for selection of these activities was that they should require the *active processing* of information. These experiences were also designed to broaden children's schematic knowledge, extend their vocabulary and, where appropriate, generate a conflict between their thinking and experience which would lead to a re-evaluation of their ideas.

The selection and design of the activities for the intervention was influenced by three factors:

(a)   A preliminary analysis of the data.

(b)   A set of ideas defined by the 'scientific' understanding (Chapter 2 - Defining Earth in Space) which would assist a child in developing an understanding of the scientific world view.

(c)   The teacher's contributions and ideas.

The elicitation gave a broad picture of the level of children's knowledge and understanding in this domain. Essentially, this had shown that there was a lack of simple observational knowledge about the daily movement of the Sun, a weakness in infant children's knowledge of time, a limited familiarity with distance and scale and a mixture of models about the movement of the Earth and Sun. Unlike some other aspects of science e.g. electricity and light, such knowledge cannot be shown or developed through empirical investigations which are a feature of much physical science. Hence, the intervention used a range of broad strategies which were available for teachers to use whenever they judged appropriate. These can be described as a) sorting activities, b) discussion activities, c) modelling/making activities, d) using secondary sources and e) simple observations and drawings. Full details of the intervention strategies suggested to teachers can be found in Appendix 3.

Sorting Activities

These activities require the active processing of information by children. Typically they would be provided with a number of cards. Each card would have the name of a planet written on it and the children were asked to sort the planets into an order such as 'largest' to 'smallest' or 'nearest to the Sun' to 'furthest from the Sun'. Teachers were also asked to provide children with ample opportunity to explore their own approaches to the categorisation of the planets such as 'hot planets' and 'cold planets', or big and small planets.

Another use of sorting was to ask children to group sets of statements about the seasons e.g. 'daffodils are out', 'snow falls' into groups to help to establish clear associations between phenomena and the seasons. An additional exercise was to use data published in the newspapers of temperatures around the World to group cities into 'cold' places and 'warm' places to see if children could see any pattern between their geographical location and the temperature.

Discussion Activities

Many of the sorting activities discussed previously were undertaken by groups and hence required discussion and communication between peers which encouraged both articulation of their own thinking and the exchange of ideas. Wherever possible, activities were used that encouraged the use of this technique.

instance, children were asked to discuss in groups sets of statements on cards ut physical phenomena such as 'The Sun goes to bed at night', 'The Sun does not ve, the Earth spins' and decide whether they firstly individually agreed or disagreed with such statements and then come to a group consensus about each statement which was later discussed with their teacher. Another suggested method of using this technique was to use historical ideas about the Earth and its movements and ask children to find evidence which supported or contradicted such statements. Possible starting points were statements of the form 'Some people think the Earth is flat and some think it is spherical' or 'Some people think the Earth goes around the Sun and others think the Sun goes around the Earth'.

Modelling/Making Activities

Models provide a tangible and concrete experience of objects which are not readily open to inspection such as the Solar System itself. Thus they are an essential aid to helping children develop an understanding of how the bodies of the Solar System might move and how these movements would account for the phenomena that we observe. Therefore activities suggested to teachers used pairs of children to represent the Sun and the Earth and asked them to act out their daily and annual movements. Such an activity can also be done for the movements of the Earth and the Moon.

Making timelines was suggested as an activity which enabled a concrete representation of time to be made. This is a useful activity for younger children to help establish the idea of 24 hours in a day, 7 days in a week and can be extended for older children into a timeline for a year of their lives and is motivational if it records their own personal experiences. The thinking was that such a simple concrete characterisation of time would help the assimilation of the arbitrary symbolic representation commonly used in our culture.

Another suggested activity was intended to provide children with an extended experience of a range of shapes and enhance their vocabulary for describing them. Children were asked to select a shape from a box and then, keeping it hidden, describe it to another child who had to guess the singular name for this shape.

The final model making activity suggested was to use torches and shadows to explore how shadow length is related to the position of the source and the size of the object. It was suggested that children be encouraged to relate this to the shadows formed by the Sun providing opportunities, whenever possible, to investigate the length and other features of such shadows.

Using Secondary Sources

Possibly more than any other domain of science, astronomical knowledge is elaborated or provided by secondary sources, typically books and posters. Teachers were therefore encouraged to assemble a collection of such resources which children could access for information. To aid children to use and record information collected in this manner, it was suggested that they be asked to keep scrapbooks or logbooks in which they could stick pictures cut out from magazines and other notes and information. Scrapbooks could either be collected on an individual, group or class basis and could be valuable as a stimulus for discussion with children.

For older children, there are strong arguments for activities which require directed reading of texts which encourage active and reflective reading. Such pieces and their associated techniques are commonly known as DARTS (Directed Activities Related to Text) and two of these were suggested to teachers as exemplars of the kind of material that could be used to assist learning from secondary sources.

Simple Observation and Drawing

Working in an urban environment, only limited observations of the night sky can be undertaken. Nevertheless, it was considered worthwhile encouraging teachers to ask children to undertake observations of the Moon on a monthly basis, particularly if these were undertaken as a class task where each child had responsibility for one night. This would help to establish an idea of the phases of the Moon and the sequence of their changes.

Drawing activities considered were the production of simple posters and mobiles of the Solar System which are an effective means of recording a large amount of data. A slightly more demanding task was to ask children to work as a group and produce a drawing of an asymmetrical object e.g. a teapot, firstly from their perspective and then from one of the other group member's perspective. Such a task requires the child to transcend their egocentricity and imagine how another sees the object. This mental process is essential to understanding the phases of the Moon and the apparent daily movement of the Sun across the sky.

General Issues

Although the data collection was undertaken by the researchers, the intervention work was undertaken by the teachers. During this phase, the researchers made regular visits to the schools to support the teachers and to share with them the data collected after the preliminary elicitation. Teachers who undertook to work on this project were given briefings about the nature of the approach and the need to elicit children's understandings of the particular concept of interest before commencing teaching. Moreover, it was emphasised to the teachers that the nature of the individual child's understanding should be the basis for determining the intervention work. That is, that they should attempt to ascertain what the child already knew before determining the strategy for teaching and learning. Sharing the data gathered from the elicitation with the individual teachers was one way of enabling this process and was undertaken in all instances. In addition, teachers were encouraged to undertake similar activities in the classroom to provide more insight for themselves.

Thus the intervention activities do not form a prescriptive list of experiences but were offered simply as a set from which selections could be made to meet the needs of the individual pupils and no attempt was made to ensure consistency of experience between one classroom and the other. Variation was inevitable and a reflection of the normal classroom realities and the variation in children. Teachers were briefed about the general approach to the intervention and the strategies to adopt and asked to offer children a wide variety of experiences and opportunities to investigate topics of interest. The briefing document which was the basis for discussion with the meetings with teachers stated:

'We suggest that you carry out at least one activity from each section[1] and then as many others as you are able to. We would like you to keep a log of all the activities which you try, noting how successful you felt they were, how the children responded and how you were able to build on the activities. It would also be helpful if you could record interesting comments made by the children and save copies of interesting/typical work.

It is important that most of the tasks stem from the children's ideas and are not presented to them in isolation. They may need to talk, write about or draw their ideas before embarking on an activity. Wherever possible, the activities should be initiated by the children in response to open-ended questions e.g. "How could we find out about....." or "How could we find if it is true?"

[1] See Appendix 3

Although children may wish to consult secondary sources for further information, this should be done in conjunction with practical activities, not "Let's look it up in a book!" first. Equipment available in the classroom for children to plan their own investigations should be a useful starting point for many of the activities.'

Consequently, the data obtained from this study cannot be used to judge the validity of any one activity but merely provide an analysis of the potential developments in children's thinking from exposure to a range of experiences which embody the broad strategies outlined here.

5: The Effects of the Intervention

This chapter provides a full analysis of the data gathered pre- and post-intervention. The data were gathered using a mixture of written questions and interviews which are provided in Appendix 2. These sets of questions evolved from a pilot phase with two groups of children. As a consequence of this experience, questions were amended or discarded and the set of questions finally used comprised a mixture - some requiring oral/ written responses, some requiring drawings and some requiring the use of simple models to provide explanations.

Classes of children were asked to write their answers to all the questions in sections A-C which included any questions that required drawings e.g. a drawing of what the Earth, Sun and Moon would look like from the window of a spaceship. Responses to all the questions in section D were obtained by individual interviews with children. The interviews made use of a set of shapes consisting of 2 large spherical balls, 2 small spherical balls, 2 large discs, 2 small discs and 2 rectangular shapes which were shown to children. Each child was then asked to select from these shapes and use them in answering the questions that followed. The child's responses were then noted by the interviewer on the sheets.

Data were gathered in two phases, an elicitation phase prior to the intervention and a further follow-up phase after the intervention. The intervention work was generally undertaken over a 'half-term' period and consequently these two phases were generally separated by a period of 6-8 weeks. The questions used in both phases were identical and had been designed to explore children's understanding using a wide range of activities which gave children the opportunity to write, talk and draw as a means of expression. In the case of infant children, all the data collection was undertaken by a process of individual interview because they could not express themselves well in writing. The data were gathered by the full-time project officer, two part-time researchers and two teachers.

The data collected explored children's understanding and their development as a consequence of the intervention designed for the Earth in Space attainment target in the then current English & Welsh National Curriculum[1]. By a process of collaborative discussion and analysis, information that answered the following questions was

---

[1]   Department of Education & Science. (1989) Science in the National Curriculum. London, HMSO. . This has now been superseded by the revised version published in 1992. In this version, Earth in Space has become a 'strand' of attainment target 4.

identified as being central to establishing a picture of the growth of children's knowledge in this domain.

1. What understanding of time do children have?

An understanding of the arbitrary divisions that constitute our notions of time was considered to be an a priori requirement for any discussion of astronomical events such as day, night, phases of the moon and seasons. Hence question 1, section A was used to ascertain whether children had grasped the normal social construction of time.

2. What do children know about the movement of the Sun through the year?

Questions here aimed to explore firstly to what extent children were aware of the difference in the altitude of the midday sun between winter and summer (Question 2, section B) and related seasonal effects (Question 1, section B). Question 1(c), section D explored children's abilities to use a model to show the relative motion of the Sun and Earth during the course of one year. Question 2, section D took this further by asking children to use the model to explain the variation in day length and temperature between summer and winter.

3. What explanations do children give for the phenomena of day and night?

Children's explanations of day and night have been the focus of many studies. This study used a range of questions to explore what children thought happened (Question 3(a), section A, Question 1 (b), section D) and why it happened (Question 3(b), section A). Questions were based on written/spoken explanations and the use of shapes, selected by the children from those provided, to demonstrate the relative movements of the Sun and Earth.

4. What do children know about the daily movement of the sun and related phenomena?

These ideas were explored through the use of question 2, section A and question 3, section B. These two questions used drawings to which children were asked to make additions in order to show the diurnal movement of the Sun and its effect on shadows. Question 4, section B was used to see if children could use any understanding they had of the Sun's daily movement to explain how a sundial works.

5. What concept of the Earth do children have?

The problem for children is to make the transition between the readily observable concept of a 'flat Earth' with a clearly delineated notion of 'down' at right angles to the two horizontal planes of the ground and the sky, and the scientific concept where 'down' is towards the centre of the Earth. Questions 1 & 2, section C and question

1(a), section D used a mixture of spoken/written explanations and drawings to investigate what kind of concept of the Earth was held by these children.

6. What is children's knowledge of distance?

One of the elements required to understand astronomy is a conception of distances. A sense of awe and the insignificance of human lifetimes and scales can only really develop from an appreciation of the enormity and grandness of the Solar System and the Universe. Hence question 4, section D asked children to provide an estimate of terrestrial and astronomical distances to provide an insight into what extent this sense of distance had been grasped and appreciated by children.

7. What knowledge of astronomical bodies do children have?

This aspect of the research explored what knowledge children had of the phases of the moon, the concept of a planet and star, and of their relative sizes. Question 5, section B simply asked children to indicate which phases of the Moon they had observed by marking a set of shapes. The second part of this question investigated whether they had any concept of the correct sequence of the phases of the Moon. Question 3, section C asked children to draw the Earth, Sun and Moon as seen from a spaceship to see if they had any concept of their relative sizes. Question 4(a), section C was a simple test of whether children were able to distinguish stars from other astronomical bodies whilst question 3, section D asked children to describe what a star was. Question 4(b), section C tested whether children could distinguish planets from other astronomical bodies and question 5, section D was a sorting activity testing if children had any conception of their comparative sizes.

The data presented here are those obtained from children who were present on all three occasions i.e. the elicitation, the intervention and the second elicitation. Full sets of data were obtained from 106 children in total. This consisted of 39 upper juniors in year 5 & 6 of their education, 31 lower juniors, in year 3 & 4 of their education and 36 infants in year 1 & 2 of their education. Sample sizes for the different age groups varied but each sample was taken from a minimum of two schools. One of the difficulties that emerges in research of this nature is the considerable diminution in the sample caused by the absence of children in one or more of these phases.

The methodology used in analysis of the data was firstly a simple categorisation of the answers and a frequency count. Categorisations were based on an empirical approach to the data from the responses provided by children. Data pre- and post-elicitation were then compared using cross-tabulations and chi-square tests to see if significant changes had occurred. Further exploration of the data was possible by investigating the data sets for significant correlations to see the extent to which children were consistent in their responses between questions. At a theoretical level, this information is important as some authors have argued that children are operating with a consistent theoretical structure, albeit a non-scientific one whereas others have argued that children's knowledge consists of a set of unrelated phenomenological primitives e.g. notions of 'support' and 'effort'. The application of the latter principles is dependent on the surface features of a problem and hence results in contextual inconsistency.

For those data where there were two or more aspects to the response i.e. in children's explanations of day and night (Section D, Q1), the data were analysed using systemic networks[2]. These networks allow for several parallel aspects of individual responses to be viewed in conjunction and present a more holistic impression of the concept that children may be using to answer elicitation questions on the same topic.

Data are conjoined through the use of one of two devices, called a 'bra' or a 'bar' respectively, for which the symbolic representations are shown below (Fig 5.1 & Fig 5.2). Fig 5.1 shows part of the network to code children's explanations of day and night. The child may explain day and night in terms of a movement of the Sun. However, in their explanations, they ascribed a wide variety of different movements to the Sun. The 'bar' in Fig 5.1 provides a simple means of categorising this wide range of alternative responses.

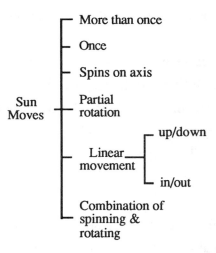

Fig 5.1 An example of a 'bar' used in systemic networks

2   Bliss J., Ogborn J. & Monk M., (1983) *Qualitative Data Analysis*. London, Croom Helm.

Each of these final categories is called a 'terminal' and counts can be made of the number of responses classified by each terminal. In addition, the network effectively represents a hierarchy and counts can be made at any level within the network. Moving further to the right on the network is said to be moving to an increasing level of delicacy.

A 'bra' is the converse in that the categories are inclusive and the different aspects of the child's response may be classified in the separate categories. Hence a child's explanations of day and night may be in terms of a movement by both the Sun and the Earth, and any analysis must include details of the movement of both bodies. The 'bra' is a device which represents such inclusive categorisation.

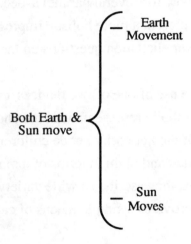

Fig 5.2: An example of a 'bra' used in systemic networks

In logic terms a 'bar' is exclusive and the response is represented by one terminal *or* another whereas a 'bra' is inclusive and the response is represented by one terminal *and* others. Such networks evolve out of an empirical process of examining the data and attempting to reflect the categories in the network. Trialling and evaluation with a cyclical process of refinement leads to the evolution of a network which is considered a 'best fit' to the data.

Each child's responses were coded using the network and then counts were made of all the responses at each terminal and analysed to see if there were significant changes as a consequence of the intervention.

1. What understanding of time do children have?

This aspect of children's knowledge was explored because a child who does not have a concept or 'feel' for what is commonly understood by a day, week or year was thought unlikely to be able to give anything more than what Piaget termed an 'artificialistic' explanation of such phenomena, i.e. night happens because God makes it happen which is in essence, the *deus ex machina* view. Hence it was hypothesised that such concepts are an a priori necessity for the development of other astronomical concepts. After some discussion of the best method of exploring such knowledge and the results of the pilot, it was decided to use a set of simple questions which asked how long a day, week and year were.

Children were asked 'How long is a day?' and provided three categories of response, 12 hours, 24 hours or no response/don't know. Table 5.1 shows the data obtained for the numbers children gave and Table 5.2 shows the data for the unit used to qualify the number.

	Inf-Pre % (n=36)	Inf-Post % (n=36)	LJ-Pre % (n=31)	LJ-Post % (n=31)	UJ-Pre % (n=39)	UJ-Post % (n=39)
12 hours	11.0	8.0	6.0	0.0	3.0	3.0
24 hours	14.0	25.0	65.0	90.0	92.0	92.0
No Response	75.0	67.0	29.0	10.0	5.0	5.0

Table 5.1: Percentage of children indicating each type of response for the different age-groups to the question 'How long is a day?'

The main features of note were the highly significant (p<0.01) distinction between infants and lower and upper juniors. The latter two groups were much better at providing a response that indicated that they had grasped the commonly accepted understanding of day length prior to the intervention. The main intervention activities suggested to develop children's understanding were based on work on timelines and sundials (Appendix 3). Although neither the improvement in the knowledge of the infant or lower juniors was significant, the overall result was that the distinction between lower juniors and infants became even more substantial (and significant).

Table 5.2 shows the data obtained for the units of time children gave in their responses. Not surprisingly, the pattern of changes between infants, lower juniors and upper juniors for the figures shown in table 5.1 and 5.2 and their significances were more or less identical. Essentially this was because of the large number of infant children who gave no response to the item and hence provided neither a figure nor a unit. However, the changes for each group between pre- and post-elicitation do differ.

	Inf-Pre %	Inf-Post %	LJ-Pre %	LJ-Post %	UJ-Pre %	UJ-Post %
Units given	36	42	81	81	87	92
Units not given	64	58	19	19	13	8

Table 5.2: Data showing percentage of children who gave units
when asked 'How long is a day?'

Clearly only a minority of infants appeared to be aware of the length of a day and the transition between the infants and the other groups is shown more dramatically by Fig 5.3. This chart also shows that the intervention has had an effect in improving the number of children who were able to give the correct response in both infants and lower junior children. Upper juniors would appear to have reached a plateau with only a very small minority who did not appear to be aware of the correct figure.

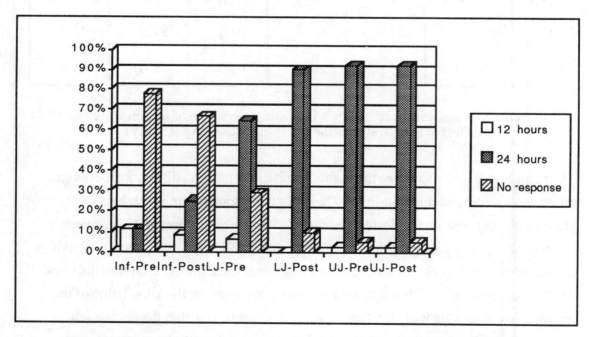

Fig 5.3. Chart of data showing the percentage of each age group giving
each type of response to the question 'How long is a day?'

Fig 5.4, 5.5 and 5.6 show the percentage of children who were able to give a correct answer respectively for the length of a day, the length of a month and the length of a year. In coding the responses to the question about the length of a month, 4 weeks, and 28-31 days were both considered acceptable responses.

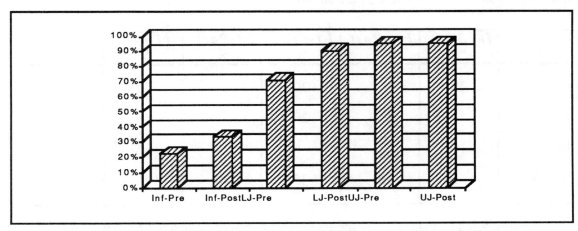

Fig 5.4. Percentage of children in each group who gave a correct answer to the question 'How long is a day?

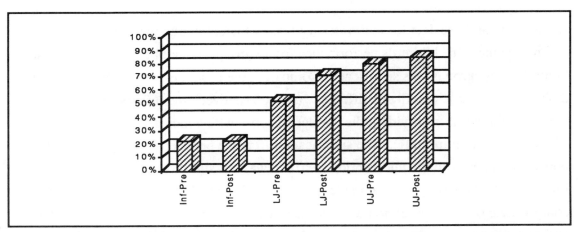

Fig 5.5: Percentage of children who gave a correct response to the question 'How long is a month?'

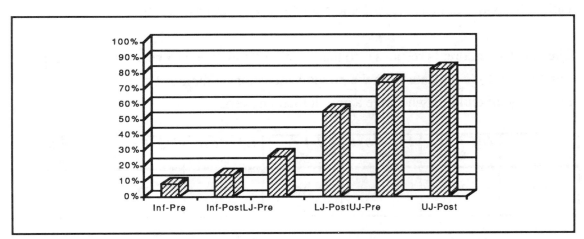

Fig 5.6: Percentage of children who gave a correct response to the question 'How long is a year?'

The figures for the units given in the children's responses e.g. day, month etc, to the question asking how long is a month were collected, irrespective of whether the numerical value was correct, and are shown in Table 5.3.

	Inf-Pre %	Inf-Post %	LJ-Pre %	LJ-Post %	UJ-Pre %	UJ-Post %
Day	19	25	29	23	21	51
Week	11	14	29	55	49	38
Both	19	22	6	3	5	3
No Unit	50	39	35	19	26	8

Table 5.3: Data showing percentage of children of each age group pre- and post-intervention who gave a unit when answering the question 'How long is a month?' (percentages have been rounded)

An analysis of these data for their responses show that, although the intervention led to an improvement in children's performance for all groups, none of the changes for the individual age groups was significant. Comparing the groupings before the intervention though, there was a significant difference ($p<0.05$) between the infants and lower juniors in the number providing the correct response which increased as a consequence of the intervention ($p<0.01$). The significant difference between lower juniors and upper juniors prior to the intervention ($p<0.05$) was not significant after the intervention. This suggests that the largest change in knowledge and understanding as a consequence of the intervention was for the lower junior group. A tentative explanation of this change might be that whilst it was fairly hard for young children to assimilate the concept of a day, let alone a month, older children were building on the concept of a day which the evidence in Tables 5.1 and 5.2 shows was already well formed.

The data for children's responses to the question 'How long is a year?' show a similar trend (Fig 5.6) to the data from the previous questions. Table 5.4 shows the percentage of children who gave a unit in their answers.

	Inf-Pre %	Inf-Post %	LJ-Pre %	LJ-Post %	UJ-Pre %	UJ-Post %
Unit	36	44	35	61	82	77

Table 5.4: Percentage of children who gave a unit in their response to the question 'How long is a year?'

Whilst it would be erroneous to treat the data shown in Figs 5.4 - 5.6 as representing a developmental curve because they show the results for three different sets of children, taken at two different times, they do depict a clear trend in children's understanding. The most obvious feature was the improvement in the number of children from pre- to post-elicitation for all age groups and, from age group to age group, who gave a correct or an approximately correct number for the length of a year. This was accompanied by a similar trend, not quite as marked, in the number who provided a unit. Both infants and lower juniors showed an improvement from pre- to post-elicitation but upper juniors effectively seemed to have reached a plateau. Both these changes are accompanied by a marked decline in the number giving no response.

A closer examination of the changes in their understanding of the concept of a year shows that the intervention led to a significant improvement in the understanding of the lower juniors ($p < 0.05$). However significant differences in understanding existed between the infants and lower juniors ($p < 0.01$) and between lower juniors and upper juniors ($p < 0.01$) prior to the intervention. Hence the major effect of the intervention would seem to have been to raise the understanding of the lower junior group.

The low facility values achieved by infants in their responses to these questions would suggest that they are not in a position to assimilate the concept of a year and the data show that there was little improvement in their understanding. On the other hand, the data also suggest that there is no need for this topic to be covered beyond the lower junior age group as the evidence shows the concepts are well-assimilated by the overwhelming majority.

It is also interesting to examine what correlations, if any, exist between those children who knew the correct answers to one question and another - the hypothesis being that those who knew about year length should be able to correctly predict the length of a day and/or a month as these are effectively sub-units of a year. Correlations were investigated to explore the extent to which those who are successful in predicting day length are also successful in predicting month or year length. The data showing the percentages who gave the correct response to each question are shown in Figs 5.7a, 5.7b & 5.7c (in brackets). In addition, the figures show the percentage who were successful on two items. Figures to the far left and right show the percentage who were successful on all three items.

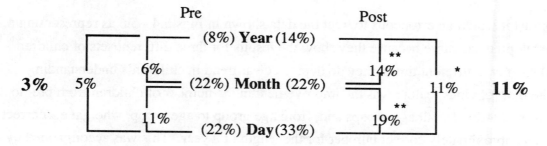

Fig 5.7a: Table showing data for infant responses and the percentages successful on one or more responses. (**, * - see text beneath).

There are several coefficients which can be calculated to measure the correlation between children's responses to these separate items of data. A simple cross-tabulation and chi-squared test gives a measure of the association between the two items and its significance. Another indicator, called the index of agreement (r_g)[3] and known as the G index, measures the extent to which children who succeed/fail on one item succeed/fail on another. The latter coefficient is useful in providing evidence of the extent to which a child's responses to two aspects are positively interrelated. If responses require the application of the same schematic knowledge, it is a reasonable hypothesis that lack of such schematic knowledge would lead to failure on both items. The calculation of a significance value using chi-squared for the relationship gives some indication of the extent to which each distribution is non-random and that there is something underpinning the relationship.

When both items fail to elicit any appropriate schema, or alternatively, when the knowledge is so well understood that the responses to both items are almost always correct, a high index of agreement will be obtained. However, where such a distribution occurs, the chi-square statistic will probably show that whilst the pattern appears non-random, it does not show significant association. The converse of this is the case when the index of agreement is high and the chi-square statistic shows a significant association. This implies that when one item is correct, there is a significant probability that the second item will be correct. The inference is that in both cases the same schema is applied. Such cases which are considered significant by the chi-squared test are shown in these diagrams with an asterisk (p<0.05) and a double asterisk (p<0.01).

---

[3]   Guilford, J.P & Fruchter, B. (1981) *Fundamental Statistics in the Psychology of Education* (6th Ed). Singapore, McGraw-Hill. The index of agreement is simply a coefficient which gives the difference between the fraction of those cases who agree on both items and those who disagree.

For the infant groups all the indexes of agreement are greater than +0.5 on a scale of total negative correlation (-1) to total positive correlation (+1). All of these high indexes prior to the intervention are explained by the large number of children who failed to answer any item successfully. After the intervention, the indexes of agreement were all in excess of +0.5 but this time the chi-square statistic showed that there was a significant non-random relationship between their responses.

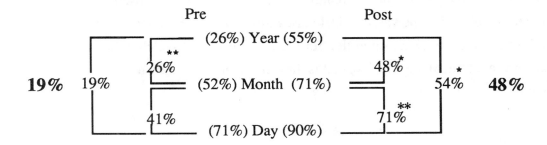

Fig 5.7b: Table showing data for lower junior responses and the percentages successful on one or more responses. (**, * - see text above).

The data for the lower juniors showed a similar pattern to that for the infants. Larger numbers of children were successful in their responses to these items and the correlations were more significant after the intervention than before, demonstrating some evidence that an appropriate schema had been developed.

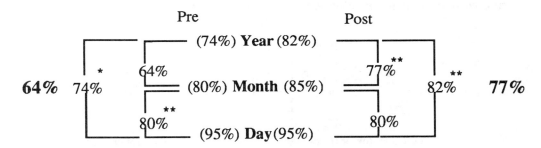

Fig 5.7c: Table showing data for upper junior responses and the percentages successful on one or more responses. (**, * - see text above).

The data for the upper juniors show a much higher level of success with responses to these items. In this case, the indices of agreement between all these items was 0.48 or greater. The high level of agreement was explained by the numbers of children who had no difficulty in replying to these items correctly so that after the intervention the relationship between responses for day length and month length has no significant association. However the data do show that there are significant relationships between day length and year length and between month length and year length after the intervention. Taken together with the data for the other two groups after the intervention, it is argued that this shows that the knowledge and understanding of these items is strongly related and interdependent i.e. that they are schematically related.

A further test, known as the Del[4] test, enables the data in a 2 x 2 contingency table to be tested to see if knowledge of day length is a pre-condition for success in answering the question about month or year length. These coefficients are shown in table 5.5. The value of Del varies from +1, which indicates that success on A is a total pre-condition for success on B, to -1 which indicates that the items are mutually exclusive, that is that failure on A is likely to lead to success on B.

A value for the significance of Del can be calculated, and in table 5.5 is shown by an * implying that the item is significant at $p<0.05$, ** implying significance at $p<.01$ and *** implying significance at $p<.001$. In reading the tables, there are two Del values provided for each item. Those indicating the dependence of the response to month length on the response to day length, the response to year

---

4   Given two items to which the children's responses can be categorised into success (1) or failure (0), the cells of interest in a 2 x 2 contingency table become those where the child succeeded on one item but failed on another i.e. cells b and c.

Item A

		0	1
I t e m	0	a	b
B	1	c	d

For instance, if cell b is low or 0, it means that success on A only happens for children who have succeeded in B so that it can be inferred that success on Item B is a pre-condition for success on item A. For instance, the following contingency table was obtained from Lower Juniors after the intervention for their responses to day length and month length.

Month

		0	1
D a y	0	3	0
	1	6	22

It shows that there were no children who succeeded in answering the question about the length of a month who had not succeeded in answering the question about day length. Conversely there are several children who are successful in answering the question about day length who fail to answer the question about the length of a month. The obvious inference from these data is that knowledge of day length is an a priori construct to understanding the concept of a month.

length on month length and the response to year length on day length lie beneath the diagonal. Hence in the post-test, the Del value of 0.7, marked with an *(a)*, is high and significant indicating that a successful response to day length is a pre-condition for a successful response to the question about year length. Whereas, the del value for the converse relationship is 0.23, marked with a *(b)* which indicates that although there is a positive relationship between the responses to these two items, it is not significant. Hence the pre-condition for answering the question about year length is a correct answer to the question about day length.

Overall, the results show that prior to the intervention, there was no relationship of any significance between the infant responses. After the intervention, many of the relationships between the responses were significant and showed that there was a clear hierarchy where a correct response to year length was dependent on knowledge of month length which in turn was dependent on a knowledge of day length.

	Pre					Post		
	Day	*Month*	*Year*			*Day*	*Month*	*Year*
Day		0.29	0.15		*Day*		0.46*	0.23[b]
Month	0.33		0.18		*Month*	0.81**		0.56**
Year	0.56	0.57			*Year*	0.70** [a]	1.0***	

Table 5.5. Table of Del coefficients for infant children's responses to day, month and year length

Table 5.6. shows the same coefficients calculated for the lower junior children. It shows a similar pattern with little or no significance in the relationships prior to the intervention which then became highly significant after the intervention.

	Pre					Post		
	Day	*Month*	*Year*			*Day*	*Month*	*Year*
Day		0.15	0.02		*Day*		0.30	0.13
Month	0.35		0.21		*Month*	0.59**		0.26
Year	0.14	1.00***			*Year*	1.00***	1.0***	

Table 5.6. Table of Del coefficients for lower junior children's responses to day, month and year length

The data for upper juniors are shown in table 5.7. These are different in that a definite significant relationship between their responses did exist prior to the intervention with a clear hierarchy indicating that these concepts were well understood. The negative relationship between day and month after the intervention with a Del value of -0.18 is accounted for by the fact that 80% of children were successful on both items, a success rate so high that there is no significant relationship between the two items.

	Pre					Post		
	Day	*Month*	*Year*			*Day*	*Month*	*Year*
Day		0.21	0.16		*Day*		-0.05	0.25
Month	1.00***		0.25		*Month*	-0.18		0.49
Year	1.00***	0.33			*Year*	1.00***	0.59**	

Table 5.7. Table of Del coefficients for upper junior children's responses to day, month and year length

Finally, a paired t-test was conducted on an overall variable constructed from the data which is a measure of those who responded correctly or nearly correctly to all of the questions about day, month and year length. This showed a significant improvement ($p<0.05$) after the intervention for the lower juniors' understanding of the general concept of time as represented by this compound variable. The changes for infants and lower juniors were not significant as infant understanding improved only marginally whilst upper juniors had substantially assimilated the concept of time and its divisions.

2.What do children know about the movement of the Sun through the year?

If children are going to develop a model to explain seasonal differences, it follows that a basic requirement is that they should be aware of typical distinctions. If not, from their perspective, there would be little apparent need to engage in an exploration or discussion of what is likely to happen to the Earth to cause such events. Two questions (Question 1 and Question 2, Section B) attempted to elicit whether children knew of common seasonal changes. Children were asked to add the Sun to a drawing of a playground to show where it would be, firstly in winter at midday, and then in summer at the same time. There were two predominant features to their responses. Firstly whether the two responses were aligned vertically or horizontally and secondly for those that showed the responses aligned vertically, whether the summer Sun was placed at a higher altitude than the winter Sun. The data for their responses are shown in table 5.8.

	Inf-Pre %	Inf Post %	LJ-Pre %	LJ-Post %	UJ-Pre %	UJ-Post %
Vertically aligned and correct	8	14	29	32	8	23
Vertically aligned and incorrect	0	8	23	16	13	28
Horizontally placed on the same level	92	78	48	52	79	49

Table 5.8: Data for children's drawings of the Sun at midday
in the summer and winter

Although the intervention has had a positive effect in improving the number who are familiar with the change in position of the Sun between summer and winter, none of the changes was significant and only a minority are capable of showing the correct relative positions. Moreover, there did not seem to be much of an apparent improvement across the age range. Collapsing the data into two groupings of 'vertical' and 'horizontal' does show that the number of upper juniors showing the Sun in different vertical positions increased and this was significant ($p<0.01$). However, the fact that only a low percentage seemed to be aware of a relatively simple observation of the variation of the Sun's altitude from winter to summer, which in itself is the basis for an explanation of the seasons, would imply that many of these children would have been incapable of giving an appropriate explanation for the cause of the seasons.

Other seasonal differences between summer and winter

Children were asked if they could think of three differences between a summer day and a winter day. Six differing responses were obtained. Summer days were hotter or vice versa, winter days were colder; people's clothing varied; summer days were longer; there were seasonal variations in foliage or plants and finally, activities were different in the summer i.e. people went on holiday, sunbathed etc. Fig 5.8 shows a summary of the children's responses indicating the percentage obtained in each category.

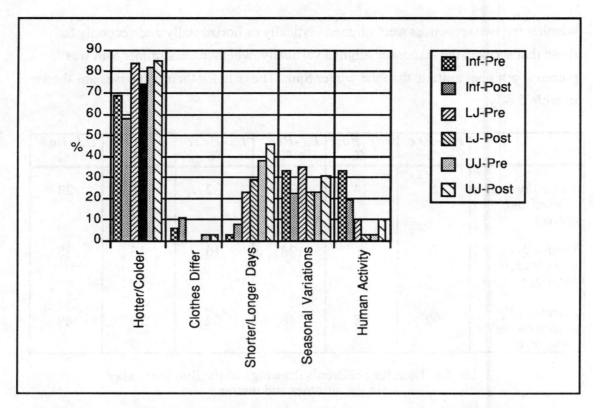

Fig 5.8: Chart showing the percentage of children giving each category of response to a question asking about seasonal differences for each age group pre- and post-elicitation.

The graph shows that the overwhelming response obtained to this question indicated that the summer/winter days were hotter/colder. Other responses were also given but by a much smaller minority of the sample. The data also show that there was little variation between any of the age groupings and between the pre- and post-elicitation with the exception of the category of answers about the length of day. Here there was a steady improvement with increasing age in the number providing this response but there were no significant changes as a result of the intervention. The difference between infants and lower juniors prior to the intervention was significant ($p<0.05$) though, as was the difference between infants and upper juniors ($p<0.01$).

What are the implications of the data in Fig 5.8 and table 5.8. Taken independently of any other data, they indicate that only the most obvious seasonal differences registered with the majority of children, and that older children showed an increasing familiarity with the variation in day length between winter and summer, but that the intervention had little effect on their knowledge of the typical variations between seasons. Clearly such information is not something which impinges on children's minds readily. If so, it is possible that explanations for the seasonal variation are likely to be of little significance and meaning since they address physical phenomena that are not assimilated, possibly because the time scale of the variation is so large in terms of children's experience as to be meaningless.

For the lower and upper junior group, the data were examined to see if there was any agreement[5] between their responses for the difference in the height of the Sun between Summer and Winter and their responses for the length of day and the variation in temperature between the seasons. The data are shown in table 5.9a & 5.9b.

		Length of Day	Seasonal Variation in Temperatures
Pre	Height of Sun (Summer /Winter)	-0.22	-0.35
Post	Height of Sun (Summer /Winter)	-0.03	0.03

Table 5.9a: Table of G indexes of agreement for responses by lower juniors to question about height of Sun (winter/summer) and variation in day length and seasonal temperatures.

		Length of Day	Seasonal Variation in Temperatures
Pre	Height of Sun (Summer /Winter)	0.28	-0.13
Post	Height of Sun (Summer /Winter)	0.13	-0.33

Table 5.9b: Table of G indexes of agreement for responses by upper juniors to question about height of Sun (winter/summer) and variation in day length and seasonal temperatures.

Calculations of Del values for both lower juniors and upper juniors show that the only relationship where there was a significant relationship was prior to the intervention for the upper juniors. For this group the data showed that knowledge of seasonal variation in temperature appeared to be a pre-condition for success in showing how the height of the Sun varied between the two seasons. However, such a relationship was not maintained after the intervention. The picture that emerges again is a lack of any defined relationship between these separate components of their knowledge. In fact the data show that there was a negative correlation between these two aspects of their knowledge in some cases. This would suggest that these children were operating with

---

5   Using r_g as a measure of the index of agreement

knowledge which is essentially fragmented and unrelated, and that knowledge of a physical phenomenon does not necessarily carry with it an understanding of a model which enables relationships and links to be made to other physical phenomena.

Data for an item which required the children to use models to explain how the Sun and Earth moved during the course of a year are shown in Fig 5.9. This chart shows the broadest features of their response divided into the categories of no response, one body moved or both bodies moved.

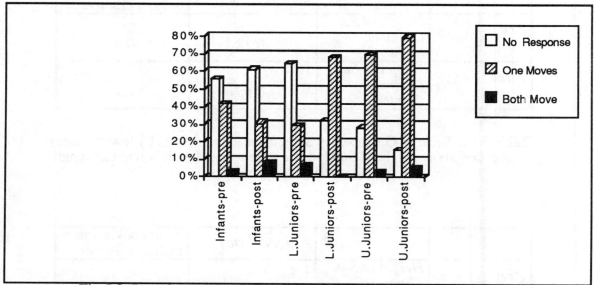

Fig 5.9: Data for children's explanation of the annual movements of the Sun and Earth.

The most noticeable feature was the significant transition that occurs as a consequence of the intervention in the understanding of the lower juniors. From a situation where the majority provided no response to this item prior to the intervention, it changed to one where the majority indicated that either the Earth or the Sun move. Thus the lower juniors improved to a position where, in broad terms, their understanding was similar to that of the upper juniors, prior to the intervention and this represented a significant change (p<0.01). None of the other changes was significant.

The data were analysed using a systemic network (Fig 5.10) which gives a picture of the range of explanations provided by children and the variation between groups. As indicated the broad division within the network is whether the child showed one or both bodies moving. Then within that, the network shows the details of the movement they ascribed to individual bodies. Whilst the network at first sight seems complex, the bottom half is really a replication of the top half to enable the categorisation of answers which stated that both bodies move. The data in Fig 5.11 show that only a minority did this. More importantly what these data show is the increasing number who provide the correct response that the Earth moves during the course of the year.

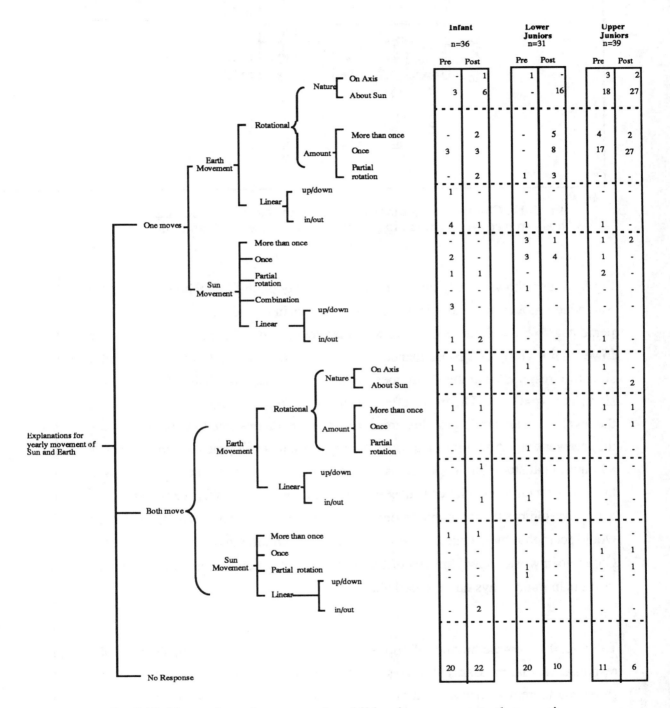

Fig 5.10: Network used to categorise children's responses to the question asking them to show with their shapes how the Earth or Sun moved during a year.

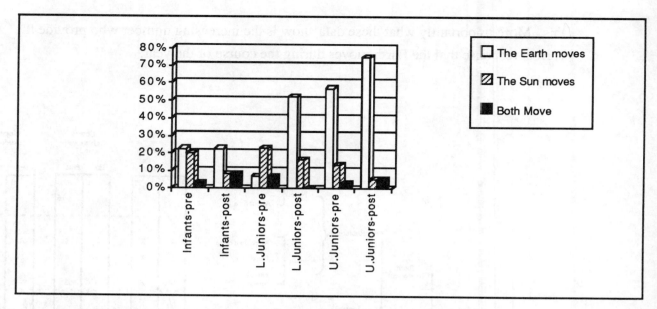

Fig 5.11: Chart showing the percentage of the children indicating which body moved when explaining what happens to the Earth and Sun during one year.

Fig 5.11 also shows clearly that there was a minority of children who thought that it is the Sun which moves and that this group only declines in the upper juniors. At all ages, the percentage who said that both move was relatively small. The main change occurred with the lower junior group as a consequence of the intervention, where the percentage who gave the scientific response that the Earth goes round the Sun rose from 6% to 52% which was significant ($p < 0.01$). The major effect of the intervention would seem to have been to raise the level of understanding of this group near to that demonstrated by the upper juniors prior to the intervention. Again the chart does not represent a developmental sequence as this was not a longitudinal study but it does at least indicate that it was children of age 8/9 years who are the youngest children who can successfully assimilate the scientific explanation. For infants and upper juniors the intervention only had marginal improvements and, for the latter group, it would seem that by the age of 10/11 the majority of children have already assimilated the Copernican world view. In view of the lack of direct concrete evidence for such a view, this result is in many ways quite remarkable.

Table 5.10 shows the number of pupils in each grouping who gave the features of a scientific response i.e. that the Earth a) moves about the Sun, and b) does so once in a year. The data show that there has been a significant ($p < 0.01$) improvement in the number of upper and lower junior children holding the Copernican world view of the annual movement of the Earth around the Sun. Also they show that the idea the Earth moves was sometimes established for younger children before a clear conception of how often it moves. In addition there is a clear correlation ($r_{g_{LJ\text{-post}}} = 0.48$; $r_{g_{UJ\text{-pre}}} = 0.89$; $r_{g_{UJ\text{-post}}} = 0.97$) between these two aspects of knowledge which in all cases was highly significant (p<0.01). This would then suggest that once the child accepts the scientific view that the Earth moves, the information about how long it takes is also assimilated at more or less the same time.

	Inf-Pre (n=36)	Inf-Post (n=36)	LJ-Pre (n=31)	LJ-Post (n=31)	UJ-Pre (n=39)	UJ-Post (n=39)
Earth moves about the Sun	3	6	0	16	18	27
Earth moves about the Sun and moves once in a year	3	3	0	8	17	27

Table 5.10: Numbers giving features of a correct scientific response in explaining how the Earth and Sun move during the course of one year.

The question then arose as to whether children were capable of using the information about how the Earth moved to explain the variation in day length and temperature with season. The question exploring this aspect of their understanding was asked in two parts. Firstly the children were asked if they could explain with their shapes or by drawing, why the day is longer in summer (Question 2(a), section D) and then, why it is hotter in summer (Question 2(b), section D). The data obtained for children's responses to the first question are shown in table 5.11. Data on this item were not collected from infants as the pilot exploration had shown that such questions had little meaning for this group of children.

	Inf-Pre %	Inf-Post %	LJ-Pre %	LJ-Post %	UJ-Pre %	UJ-Post %
Partial Scientific Explanation	-	-	0	19	21	49
Scientifically incorrect	-	-	61	48	46	28
No response/ Don't Know	-	-	45	32	33	23

Table 5.11: Data summarising the nature of children's explanations with models for why the day length varies throughout the year.

In this area, the suggested intervention activities to explore children's understanding were based around discussion of simple propositions about the movement of the Sun and Earth and a set of activities asking children to act out the movement of the Sun and Earth. Children's responses were categorised in three groups - those that showed a partial scientific explanation in that they mentioned that the Earth is tilted or that the Sun is higher in the sky; those that were scientifically incorrect, and those that gave no response. The results show that the number of children providing an explanation mentioning aspects of the full scientific explanation increased as a consequence of the intervention and both sets of changes were significant ($p<0.05$). Some of these explanations were the full scientific explanation making good use of their model to show that the earth's axis is tilted which results in an enhanced day length for half the year and diminished day length for the other half. However such explanations were relatively rare and have therefore not been counted separately.

Cross-tabulations of children's explanations for why day length varies with their models for the motion of the Sun through the year showed that a) there was a significant relationship between the two ($p<0.05$) both pre- and post-intervention and that b) success at explaining the variation was dependent on assimilating a Copernican model of how the Sun moves during the course of a year ($p<0.05$). The implication of this for teachers is that the Copernican model is an essential pre-requisite to developing an explanation of the variation between seasons.

The second part of this question asked children if they could use their models to explain why it is hotter in summer than in winter. The data for children's responses were categorised into four groupings: those that explained that the Sun was nearer in summer; those that used climatic reasons e.g. the Sun is hotter in summer which is essentially a tautology; those that were unable to explain or gave no response and those that gave other reasons. The data for their responses are shown in Table 5.12.

	Inf-Pre %	Inf-Post %	LJ-Pre %	LJ-Post %	UJ-Pre %	UJ-Post %
Sun nearer	-	-	55	68	44	56
Climatic	-	-	23	16	23	13
No Response/ Don't Know	-	-	23	16	28	28
Other	-	-	0	0	5	3

Table 5.12: Data summarising the nature of children's explanations with models for why the days are warmer in summer.

The main feature of the data was a lack of any change from one group to another as a consequence of the intervention. The naturalistic explanation that the rise in temperature in the summer is due to the closer proximity of the Sun predominated, as it does notably with adults.

This is clearly an idea with an inherently powerful logic which appeals to intuition. Furthermore, the scientific explanation requires the appreciation and understanding of three factors: the annual movement of the Earth round the Sun; the tilt of the Earth's axis and the effect of the combination of the latter on the insolation (energy received per m^2) on the ground. Therefore, it was not surprising that the scientific explanation was not offered by any children and that even adults find it difficult to articulate. The results would indicate that either this concept should be left out of any formal teaching within the primary school or, alternatively, only aspects of the explanation should be dealt with i.e. the annual movement of the Earth or the tilt of its axis but that the combination of the three is conceptually too difficult.

3. What explanations do children give for the phenomena of day and night?

Two questions were used to elicit the explanations that children gave for the origin of day and night. The first question (Question 3(a), section A) simply asked children what happened to the Sun at night. The explanations were categorised into the following groups: simple explanations which stated that the Sun goes down; those which said that the Sun moves round to the other side; explanations which said that the Earth moves or turns on its axis and explanations which said that the Moon/clouds cover the Sun. 6% of lower juniors prior to the elicitation also gave no response. A summary of the data is shown in Fig 5.12 (a) & 5.12 (b)

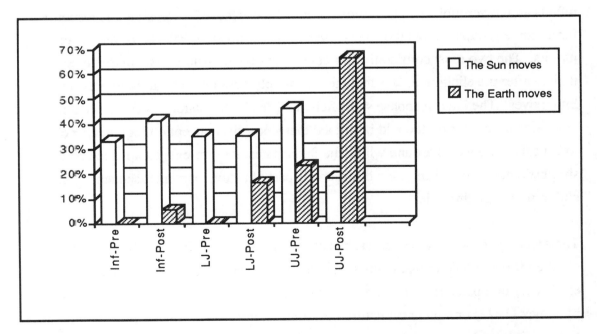

Fig 5.12a: Chart showing percentage of children indicating which body moved in response to question asking what happens to the Sun at night.

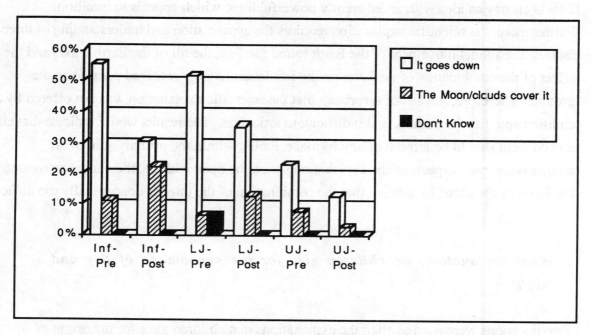

Fig 5.12 (b): Chart showing percentage of children giving other responses
to the question asking what happens to the Sun at night.

Fig 5.12 (b) reveals some quite interesting trends in children's responses. Firstly the number giving the typical response found by Piaget, that clouds cover the Sun, was a minority. Whilst this response was greatest with the infant children, it never exceeded 25% and steadily declined. The number who indicated the scientific view, that the Earth turns on its axis (Fig 5.12 (a)), was zero prior to the elicitation for both the infants and lower juniors. The intervention had the effect of increasing this response for all three groups though the change was only significant (p<0.01) for the upper juniors. The two most commonly expressed ideas by all groups, except the upper juniors after the elicitation, was that the Sun simply goes down or alternatively, that the Sun moves. The latter response was often qualified by the statement that it went to the other side of the Earth. It could be argued that since this conception requires the child to conceive of a world around which the Sun rotates, it represents an advance on the simplistic notion of a Sun going down and is part of a developmental sequence that children may go through.

The second part of this question probed children's answers a little further by asking children if they could explain why night happens. Responses to this question were essentially of a personal nature i.e. 'so that I can go to sleep' which have been reported by Piaget (1929) or a physical nature i.e. 'because the Earth spins away from the Sun'. Some children also gave no response. The data for their responses are shown in Table 5.13.

The egocentric personal response diminishes across the age groupings although the intervention has had little effect in changing such responses from the infant grouping where over two thirds provide such a response. This general trend was accompanied by an increase in the number of children who gave a response based in physical phenomena and the intervention has had a significant effect ($p<0.05$) for both the lower and upper juniors in improving the number who provided this response. Significant differences did exist prior to the intervention between the responses of the infants and the upper juniors to this question. The outcome of the intervention has been to increase the differences in their understanding so that the lower juniors attained one similar to the upper juniors whilst the infants' understanding remained static. Hence the distinction between the infants and the other two groups' answers after the intervention had become highly significant ($p<0.01$).

	Inf-Pre %	Inf-Post %	LJ-Pre %	LJ-Post %	UJ-Pre %	UJ-Post %
Personal	64	75	42	29	38	26
Physical	14	14	23	52	44	69
Don't Know/ No response	22	11	35	19	18	5

Table 5.13: Data for children's explanations for why night happens.

Children were also asked to use the models they had selected to represent the Sun and the Earth (Question 1(b), section D) to show what happens during one day and night. A wide variety of responses was obtained. These were analysed using a systemic network shown in Fig 5.13.

Table 5.14 shows the nature of children's responses at the most general level of categorisation in the network i.e. the categories on the left-hand side. At this level, the main feature of interest is how many children gave explanations which indicated only one body moved. The data show that such children were in a majority, even with the infant children, and that the numbers giving such an explanation improved with the intervention and across the age range. The change for the lower juniors was significant ($p<0.05$).

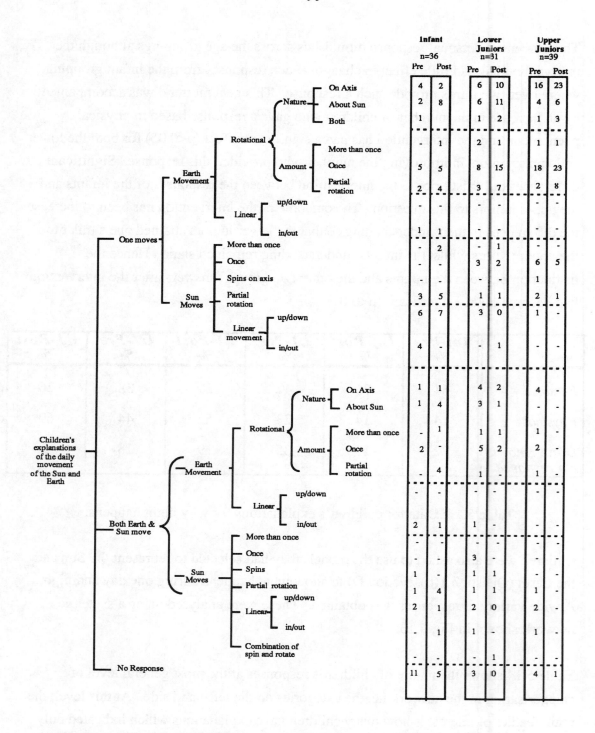

Fig 5.13: Network for the analysis of children's explanations using models of how the Sun/Earth or both move in one day and night.

	Inf-Pre %	Inf-Post %	LJ-Pre %	LJ-Post %	UJ-Pre %	UJ-Post %
One Moves	58	69	65	90	79	97
Both Move	11	17	26	10	10	0
No Response	31	14	10	0	10	3

Table 5.14: Data for children's responses using models to explain how day
and night happens.

Moving to the next level of delicacy, Fig 5.14 shows the percentage of children who gave the scientific response that it is the Earth that moves and the other attributes of the scientific explanation i.e. that it spins on its axis and rotates once.

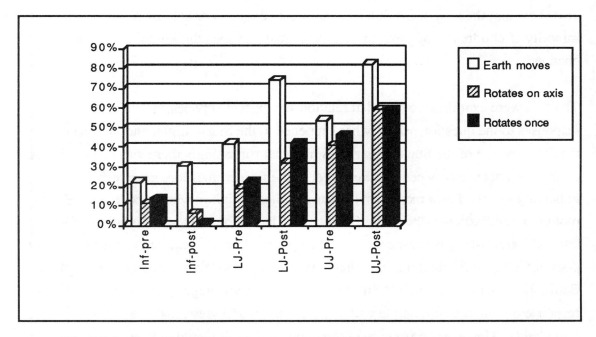

Fig 5.14: Chart showing the percentage of children who gave the response
that it is the Earth which moves and other attributes of the scientific
explanation for the phenomena of day and night.

The data show that there was a change in the numbers indicating that it is the Earth which moves and positive increases in this response for all groups as a consequence of the intervention. For both the lower and upper juniors, these changes were highly significant (p<0.01). The numbers giving the full attributes of the scientific explanation, that the Earth spins and spins on its axis once, increased from 36% to 46% for the upper juniors (p<0.01), from 10% to 19% for the lower juniors and only the infants group showed a decrease in the number of children giving aspects of the scientific response after the intervention from 8% to 6%. Infants who did say that the Earth moved predominantly stated that it moved about the Sun and this response would suggest that there was an unresolved confusion in their minds. The intervention had introduced the idea that the Earth moves but either the daily and annual movements were confused, or the idea that the Earth moves about the Sun was acceptable to these children in providing an explanation for the apparent motion of the Sun. Hence what the data show is the possibility that such children were operating with proto-concepts, that is concepts which are an amalgam of aspects of detail from a wide range of sources.

The major response that infant children gave was the naturalistic explanation that it is the Sun which moves. However, the data show that by the age of 8/9 this was not the dominant explanation and the idea that it was the Earth that moved had become the predominant explanation offered by lower juniors prior to the intervention. The data also show that the idea of the Sun moving was maintained or held by a significant minority of children throughout the age range and that such thinking was not easily changed.

The data were examined to see what relationship existed between the children's responses to the question asking what happened to the Sun at night, and their models of the daily motion of the Sun and Earth. Somewhat surprisingly there was no correlation of any significance between children who, in the former question, gave responses indicating that the Earth moved on its axis and those children whose model of the daily motion of the Earth was the scientific one. Similarly there was no correlation between those children who gave responses based on physical phenomena to the question 'Why does night happen?' and those who held the scientific model of the daily motion of the Earth. In the case of the infant children, such small percentages gave either a physical response or a model compatible with the scientific world view, that this is not remarkable. However, in the case of the upper juniors, it would indicate that the items are seen as separate items of knowledge with little or no interdependence.

4. What do children know about the daily movement of the Sun and related phenomena?

This is an aspect of knowledge expected from children by the National Curriculum. In addition, it is one of the simplest phenomena to observe and must be applied to explain the workings of a simple sundial. The research therefore attempted to investigate what knowledge children had of this everyday phenomenon and whether they could apply it in explaining how the sundial actually worked.

The first question (Question 2, section A) utilised a drawing to which children were asked to add a drawing of the Sun on their way to school, at midday and on the way home from school. The drawing is shown in Appendix 2 and reflects the typical environment of the pupils who were the subject of this study. Children's drawings show two aspects of particular interest, the sequence in which they place their position of the Sun, e.g. left to right or alternatively right to left, and the level of the Sun above the horizon. The possible responses are best summarised by a simple network shown in Fig 5.15.

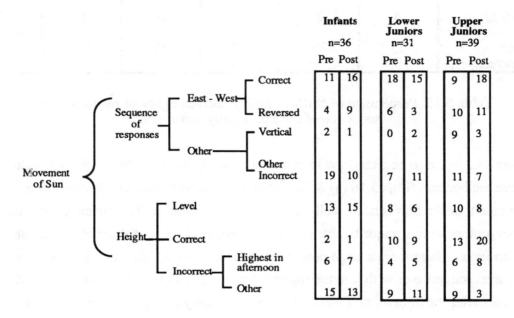

Fig 5.15: Network for analysis of children's drawings to show the position of the Sun during the day.

The data for the component of children's responses dealing with sequence are also shown in Table 5.15. The most noticeable features of the data are twofold; firstly, the lack of any really clear improvement in children's knowledge and understanding of the correct sequence and secondly, the fact that it was generally a minority of children who were capable of showing the correct sequence. Both the infants and upper juniors did show an improvement in their knowledge and the change for the latter group was significant (p<0.05) but the lower juniors' understanding seems to have regressed. A contingency table analysis of the lower juniors' responses pre-intervention against those post-intervention shows that only 23% of the sample consistently gave the correct drawing of the sequence of the daily motion of the Sun. The remaining variation was accounted for by the large number of children who moved from providing an erroneous view pre-intervention to the correct drawing post-intervention and vice versa. In addition there were a small number who were confused about the correct sequence.

For upper juniors, the number giving a correct drawing of the sequence, pre- and post-intervention was even lower at 10% and this means that the intervention may have led to the improvement of 36% in the number of upper juniors giving the correct response.

Sequence	Inf-Pre %	Inf-Post %	LJ-Pre %	LJ-Post %	UJ-Pre %	UJ-Post %
Correct	31	44	58	48	23	46
Reversed	11	25	19	10	26	28
Vertical	6	3	0	6	23	8
Other incorrect	53	28	23	35	28	18

Table 5.15: Percentage of children giving each category of response for the sequence of the Sun's daily movement.

These data needs to be examined in conjunction with those for the height of the Sun above the horizon (Figs 5.16 (a) & 5.16 (b)) which tend to confirm that the daily movement of the Sun is not a well-understood phenomenon. For instance, only for the upper juniors were a majority able to show the correct height of the midday sun above the horizon. There were a large percentage of responses which either showed the Sun in a level sequence or with it in the highest position late in the afternoon. None of the changes after the intervention were significant and only the upper juniors showed a marked improvement in their understanding. These data would suggest that the difficulty of this topic may have been underestimated and had not been fully addressed by the intervention.

Table 5.16 shows the percentage of children who gave the correct response for the sequence of the Sun's daily movement and for the height above the horizon. It would seem that the success rate on this item is surprisingly low, given that a correct response is simply dependent on observation and assimilation of a daily phenomenon. Infants were notably weaker than lower or upper juniors and only a very small minority were consistently able to correctly respond to this item in both the pre- and post-elicitation. The positive effect of the intervention was to significantly improve the understanding of this event for the upper juniors although with only 31% obtaining the correct result after the intervention.

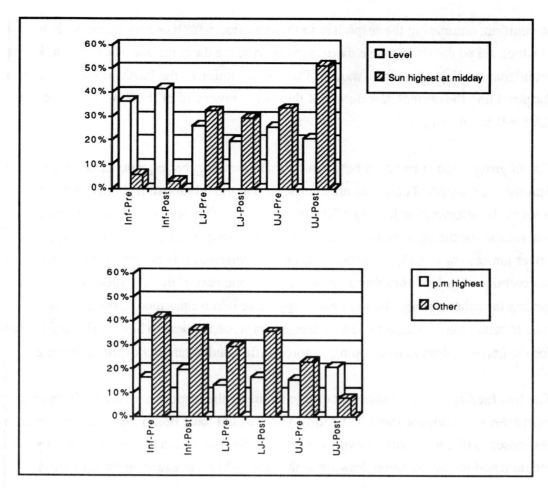

Fig 5.16 (a) & 5.16 (b): Charts showing percentage of children providing each type of response for the height of the Sun during the day.

An analysis of the data shows that for the upper juniors the change in the number of children who were able to provide the correct description of the Sun's daily movement was just significant ($p<0.05$).

	Inf-Pre %	Inf-Post %	LJ-Pre %	LJ-Post %	UJ-Pre %	UJ-Post %
Correct Sequence and Correct Height	6	3	20	23	10	31
% giving same result pre- and post-intervention		3		10		8

Table 5.16: Data showing percentage of children in each age group who were able to show the correct sequence and correct relative heights for the Sun's daily movement.

In addition, comparing the responses to this question with those for question 1, section D which asked the child to use models to describe the daily motion of the Earth, it was found that holding a scientific model of the daily motion of the Earth was a precondition for providing the correct description of the daily movement of the Sun across the sky (Del = 0.54, p<.01).

For all groups, the correlation between their answers for the sequence and height of the Sun was calculated. There was no significance in the relationships between the two prior to the intervention for any of the groups. After the intervention, there was a correlation for the upper juniors ($r_g = 0.28$, just failing significance at $p<0.05$) and the lower juniors ($r_g = 0.35$, $p <0.05$). The lack of correlation between the two prior to the intervention clearly shows that a child could get one part of this question correct whilst getting the other wrong. This is again suggestive of a fragmented knowledge which fails to relate the two aspects. The intervention would appear to have had some success for the upper juniors in developing a more unified understanding of this phenomenon.

The low facility and the somewhat erratic nature of the responses obtained from this item raise some doubts about its validity and it would have been interesting to compare responses to this item with drawings added to a flat horizon to explore the validity of the item and to use the same drawing with rural children to examine its reliability.

A knowledge of the daily movement of the Sun is necessary to predict and explain the appearance and behaviour of shadows throughout the day. The data in table 5.17, 5.18 and Fig 5.17 would suggest that children would have difficulty in making accurate predictions about the length of the shadows. To explore this children were given a drawing showing the Sun, a tree and its shadow early in the morning. They were then asked to add to this to show the position of the shadow at midday (Question 3, section B). The response had essentially two attributes of interest, the position of the shadow and its length. The full features of the response can be represented with a network.

The main feature of the position of the shadow was whether it was shown attached to the base of the tree or separate and unattached from it. Some children did show the shadow attached but at such a point that it could not be considered correct. The full data obtained from this question are shown in table 5.17.

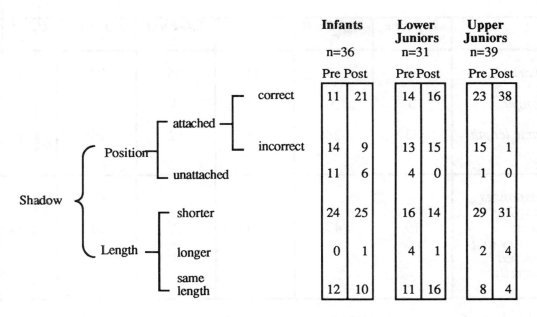

Shadow				Infants n=36 Pre	Infants n=36 Post	Lower Juniors n=31 Pre	Lower Juniors n=31 Post	Upper Juniors n=39 Pre	Upper Juniors n=39 Post
Position	attached	correct		11	21	14	16	23	38
		incorrect		14	9	13	15	15	1
	unattached			11	6	4	0	1	0
Length	shorter			24	25	16	14	29	31
	longer			0	1	4	1	2	4
	same length			12	10	11	16	8	4

Fig 5.17: Network used for the analysis of children's responses about the length of the shadow.

What the data show is that in all cases the intervention resulted in an improvement in the number correctly answering the question and this change was significant for the infants ($p<0.05$) and the upper juniors ($p<0.01$). However, only the upper juniors after the intervention activities seem to have really understood the correct position for placing the shadow.

	Inf-Pre %	*Inf-Post* %	*LJ-Pre* %	*LJ-Post* %	*UJ-Pre* %	*UJ-Post* %
Attached Correctly	31	58	45	52	59	97
Attached Incorrectly	39	25	42	48	38	3
Unattached	31	17	13	0	3	0

Table 5.17: Data for position of shadow in children's drawings to show what happened to shadow length.

Table 5.18 shows the data for the length of the shadow. The data here are less conclusive. Firstly no significant changes have occurred as a consequence of the intervention and secondly, whilst infants and upper juniors were both relatively successful at showing the midday shadow as being shorter than the morning one, the performance of the lower junior group was inferior.

	Inf-Pre %	Inf-Post %	LJ-Pre %	LJ-Post %	UJ-Pre %	UJ-Post %
Shorter	67	69	52	45	74	79
Longer	0	3	13	3	5	10
Same length	33	28	35	52	21	10
Responses showing shorter shadow and attached correctly	19	42	19	22	51	74

Table 5.18: Percentage of children giving specific lengths of shadow by age groups and the percentage giving all the features of the correct response.

Some other interesting aspects of the children's understanding emerge from examining the correlations between the data. Data for children who correctly indicated that the shadow would be shorter were correlated with data for the drawing of the movement of the Sun during the day. None of these correlations was significant although it was found that in the case of the upper juniors, the correct response to the question about the shadow was a prior requirement for the correct response to the question on the daily movement of the Sun (Del =0.68, p<0.01). These results are somewhat surprising as it would be expected that children who knew that the Sun was higher at midday would be able to reason that the shadow would be shorter at midday. These results suggest that most children do not use the relationship between the two.

The performance of the infant group is also surprising given their weakness in predicting the correct height of the Sun at midday (Fig 5.16) and it is surmised that the explanation of their performance must lie elsewhere, possibly in the lack of a full sense of perspective and proportion which limits their ability to draw and represent reality and which results in the production of a foreshortened shadow. If this is true, then it was only the upper juniors who really show a significant understanding of what the relative shadow length should be and the intervention has done little to improve their knowledge. This would mean also that the concept of the sundial and how it works, would only really be understood by the majority of children of age 10/11.

Some evidence to support this last hypothesis comes from the responses to Question 4, section B where children were asked to explain how we can use shadows to tell the time. Answers fell into those that were generally valid in that they mentioned using the shadow of the Sun; those that simply stated 'use a sundial'; a group of other responses which mentioned a wide variety of non-relevant points and those that did not answer or said they did not know. Table 5.19 shows the data obtained for this question and shows that the number of generally correct answers was limited to a maximum of 26% for the lower juniors in the post-elicitation. It was only in the upper junior group after the intervention that a large number of responses mentioned a sundial and even then, no explanation of how it works was given. Hence the total picture presented by the data is not clear but would suggest that this concept may pose particular difficulty for children below the age of 10/11.

	Inf-Pre %	Inf-Post %	LJ-Pre %	LJ-Post %	UJ-Pre %	UJ-Post %
Generally Valid	14	14	16	26	10	21
Don't Know	58	61	52	48	62	18
With a Sundial	3	3	3	10	18	51
Other	25	22	29	16	10	10

Table 5.19: Four categories of response of how a sundial could be used to tell the time and the percentage of children in each group giving each response.

For all the groups, the following relationships were explored to see if there was any correlation between the children's reasoning.

- Children's explanations of how we can tell the time from shadows *with* correct responses to the daily movement of the Sun across the sky.

  No correlations of any significance were found for any of the groups.

- Children's explanations of how we can tell the time from shadows *with* correct responses of the height of the midday sun.

  No correlations of any significance were found for any of the groups.

- Children's explanations of how we can tell the time from shadows *with* responses indicating that midday shadows will be shortened.

A significant negative correlation ($r_g = -0.35$, $p<0.05$) was found between these two variables for the lower juniors prior to the intervention. After the intervention, the correlation was still negative but just failed to be significant. For both the upper juniors and infants prior to the intervention, and the infants post-intervention, it was found that a knowledge of a shorter shadow at midday was a precondition for a correct answer on the use of a sundial for measuring time (Del = 1, $p<0.01$).

Again the surprising feature of these data was the lack of any evidence of a consistent response which would demonstrate that children were operating with a coherent model which related shadow length, the principle of a sundial and the daily movement of the Sun. Instead again their knowledge would appear to consist of fragmented and different ideas bearing little relation to each other. This finding would appear to directly contradict the work of Vosniadou & Brewer (1991) who argue that their data support the view that children are operating with a consistent theoretical structure, albeit a non-scientific one.

5.What concept of the Earth do children have?

The 'Earth' concept is an important idea which has to be assimilated in order to understand explanations of day and night and the seasons. It is also recognised as being a difficult idea to comprehend as a child's experience of everyday life tends to reinforce the idea that we live between two flat planes bounded by the Earth and the sky. Hence one of the purposes of the research was to examine to what extent children held a 'flat Earth' conception of the Earth or had assimilated the round Earth spherical concept. Children's understanding was explored with three questions, the first of which showed children a selection of shapes consisting of a sphere, disc, semi-sphere, semi-circular disc and rectangle and asked them which they felt is most shaped like the Earth. The results are shown in table 5.20.

The data are interesting in showing that the conception of the Earth as a sphere was held by the majority of children from age 5 upwards and that this percentage increased steadily with age. The other predominant shape was a disc which was chosen by a diminishing percentage as children became older. It is possible that the disc represents an attempt to reconcile the experience of flatness with the picture of roundness presented in the media and elsewhere. Children were asked why they selected the chosen shape but unfortunately, this question failed to elicit a response that provided any insights into their thinking. Responses tended to be predominantly simple descriptions such as "because it's round, not flat" or "because it's round and flat" and further probing was not undertaken.

	Inf-Pre %	Inf-Post %	LJ-Pre %	LJ-Post %	UJ-Pre %	UJ-Post %
Sphere	69	81	81	94	92	97
Disc	28	14	10	6	8	3
Semi-circle	0	3	0	0	0	0
Semi-sphere	0	0	0	0	0	0
Rectangle	3	3	10	0	0	0

Table 5.20: Percentage of children choosing each type of shape when asked which one was most shaped like the Earth.

A second chance to choose a shape to represent the Earth and the Sun was provided in question 1, section D where children were offered a wide variety of shapes i.e. spheres, discs, rectangles and semi-circles of two different sizes and asked to pick one to represent the Earth and one to represent the Sun.

	Inf-Pre %	Inf-Post %	LJ-Pre %	LJ-Post %	UJ-Pre %	UJ-Post %
2 spheres, Sun larger	28	47	32	61	54	82
2 spheres identical size	17	14	10	3	0	8
2 spheres, Sun smaller	17	14	19	16	28	8
Sphere & Disc	22	14	39	13	15	3
2 Discs, sun larger	17	11	0	3	3	0
Disc (Sun) & Square	0	0	0	3	0	0

Table 5.21: Data for choices made by children of shapes to represent the Sun and the Earth (percentages).

The data show a similar trend to that shown in Table 5.20 though the percentage making the scientific choice was not so high. In addition, there were clear improvements pre- and post-intervention in the number of children making such a choice and these changes were significant for the lower juniors (p<0.05) and upper juniors (p<0.01).

The next question used an item from previous research which asked children to add to a drawing of the Earth to show how a ball would fall at three positions which could effectively be described as the North Pole, the Equator and Australia. A strong case has been advanced that this item reveals those children whose concept of a round Earth does not extend to the world in which they live. For these children, 'down' is an absolute notion defined in terms of the horizontal planes of the earth and sky and is represented by the bottom of the page. Thus they will show the balls falling vertically towards the foot of the page. Hence this item was used to test further and explore what children's latent conceptions might be for the nature of the Earth. The data for children's responses to this item are shown in Fig 5.18 and the data were categorised into 5 groups: responses showing the ball falling vertically down; responses showing the ball emerging radially outwards; responses showing the ball falling radially inwards either to the surface or to the centre of the Earth and other responses which were not simply codeable. The latter responses tended to be ones showing the ball projected horizontally around the Earth or simply no response.

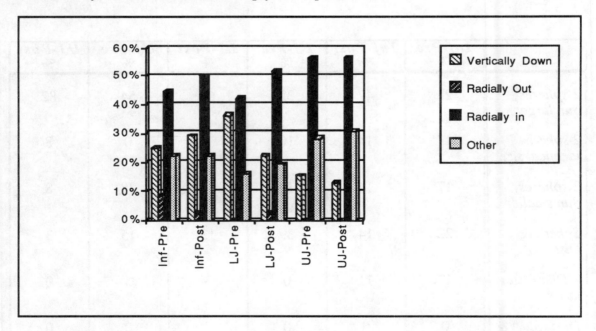

Fig 5.18: Chart showing percentage of each type of response by age group

The most noticeable aspect of the data was that the majority of the children show the ball falling radially in towards the centre of the Earth. This result is somewhat surprising as it contrasts strongly with the results reported by Nussbaum and Novak[6] which would indicate that only about 20% of pupils of age 10/11 would be expected to give that response as opposed to the figure of approximately 45% obtained in this research. However, Nussbaum and Novak used more than this single item to determine children's conception of the Earth and it is possible that too much can be read into one response. Nevertheless it is an effective instrument for quickly exploring typical conceptions held by children. For instance, the responses which show the ball falling vertically down reveal that there was a significant group of children who hold the 'Flat Earth' conception with the consequence that objects were represented as falling towards the bottom of the page.

None of the changes that occurred over the period of the intervention was found to be significant. However there was an improvement in the number of infants and lower juniors showing the ball falling radially, accompanied by a diminishment in the number of lower and upper juniors showing the ball falling vertically down towards the bottom of the page.

The data were examined to see if there was any correlation between the shapes that children chose for the Earth and the answers they gave to the question about the direction of fall of a ball on the Earth. Answers to the latter question which showed the ball falling to the surface or to the centre of the Earth were considered to indicate a knowledge of the scientific view.

The only index of agreement between successful responses to these two items which approached significance was for the upper juniors where $r_g = 0.33$. The figures for all the other groups showed that there is little correlation between these two responses and calls into question whether children do perceive the two questions as related and deploy the same knowledge in answering the question.

6. What is children's knowledge of distance?

Much of the sense of wonder and fascination that comes from studying astronomy depends on a conception of size and distance. Only the individual who is able to make sense of the distances and scale of the Solar System and the Universe will begin to appreciate how small is the world on which we live. Hence this research examined the

---

[6]   Nussbaum, J. & Novak, J.D. (1976) An Assessment of Children's Concepts of the Earth Utilizing Structured Interviews, *Science Education*, 60, (4), 535-550.

extent to which a sense of terrestrial and astronomical distances had been grasped and appreciated by children in the lower and upper juniors. This task was not undertaken with infants as the pilot had shown that such a task had little meaning for them.

Their understanding was elicited by the use of a sorting activity (Question 4, section D) which asked children to place 6 cards, each with the name of an object or town written on it, in order of the largest distance from London first. Written on the cards were Sun, New York, Moon, Mars[7], Liverpool and Southend. Children were given an opportunity to undertake the sorting activity and their results classified by whether the order was correct, whether one card was misplaced or whether their sequence was essentially incorrect showing no real awareness of the relative sizes.

	LJ-Pre %	LJ-Post %	UJ-Pre %	UJ-Post %
Correct	10	29	21	33
One Item misplaced	42	26	46	38
Incorrect	48	45	33	28

Table 5.22: Data for children's ability to correctly sort a sequence of 6 distances by order.

In both groups of children, the intervention has improved the number who were capable of performing the task correctly though none of the changes was significant. If the figures for the number getting one item misplaced are collapsed with those obtaining the correct answer, then it would seem that at least half of the pupils in the 8-11 age range were capable of undertaking this task correctly or nearly so. However, this task only really provides information about whether children have established a relative scale of distance.

Hence to explore if any children had an absolute scale of distance, the next part of this question asked children to tell the interviewer how far it was to each of the places on the card. The children's responses essentially had three aspects of interest - whether they gave a number, whether the answers were very approximately correct, loosely interpreted as any figure within plus or minus 100% of the real figure, and then

---

[7]   If Mars is on the other side of the Sun to the Earth, it will in fact be further away from the Earth than the Sun. However, it was not expected that children of this age would be able to operate with such reasoning and instead would use the standard picture of the linear presentation of the planets where Mars is much nearer to the Earth than the Sun. This was also a reason for considering those responses that had just one item misplaced.

whether they were consistent in their use of units. The data obtained are as shown in Table 5.23. These show firstly that only a very small number of lower juniors and a slightly larger number of upper juniors were capable of providing an answer that was even very approximately correct. A much larger number of children added a unit to their answer which shows at least a linguistic familiarity with the convention for expressing distances. However, the number doing so is erratic, particularly in the case of the lower juniors where it seems to have gone down dramatically after the intervention for no apparent reason and this was the only change of significance ($p<0.01$).

	LJ-Pre %	LJ-Post %	UJ-Pre %	UJ-Post %
Units given	71	35	49	59
No units	6	6	3	10
Approximately Correct	3	3	10	10
Incorrect	74	39	41	59
Don't Know	23	58	49	31

Table 5.23: Data for children's responses to question asking for distances to 6 specified places.

What the data do show is that very few children had any sense of distance to many of these places. This would imply that any sense of scale of the Solar System may be beyond the grasp of many children.

The final part of this section was a question which attempted to find out if children had a sense of the relative size of some of the the different bodies in the Solar System. This was done by providing children with six cards with the names written on (Sun, Moon, Earth, Jupiter, Mars, Saturn) and asking them to sort them by size. Responses were grouped into those that were all correct; those that were correct bar one; those that had the Sun, Earth and Moon in the correct order and those that were incorrect. The results are shown in table 5.24.

	LJ-Pre %	LJ-Post %	UJ-Pre %	UJ-Post %
All objects in correct sequence	0	19	33	38
All but one in correct sequence	6	6	3	10
Sun, Earth & Moon in correct sequence	23	26	3	21
Incorrect	71	48	62	31

Table 5.24: Data for children's responses to question asking children to sort 6 astronomical objects by size.

The data show that for both groups there was an increase in the number who got the sequence or all bar one correct. The change for lower juniors was significant (p<0.05) as was the decrease in the number of upper juniors failing to give a response in the first three categories (p<0.01). After the intervention about 50% of lower juniors and 70% of upper juniors were capable of providing some meaningful response in that their answer fell in one of the first three categories which did imply that they had some sense of scale of these bodies and that it was possible to develop children's knowledge of this aspect of the Solar System.

The number succeeding totally and the number succeeding with only one mistake were collapsed to form one data item. This process was repeated for the previous sorting task and the two compared in a contingency table. This revealed that success on the task of sorting a set of cards with a range of place names on them was significantly correlated (p<0.05 - upper juniors, p<0.01 - lower juniors), after the intervention, with success on the task of sorting the set of cards for the planets, Moon and Sun for both the lower juniors ($r_g = 0.33$) and upper juniors ($r_g = 0.42$). This would suggest that such pupils have developed a sense of scale which is applied as a common criterion to both tasks. The Del coefficients indicated that success on the first task of sorting distances is a prior condition for success on the second task of sorting the Sun, Moon and Earth and planets by size. For the lower juniors, the Del coefficient was 1.0 (p<.001) and for the upper juniors it was 0.63 (p<0.001). The other Del coefficients for success on the task of sorting the planets, Moon, Sun and Earth being dependent on success in sorting the distances were not significant. This would indicate that an understanding of the relative sizes of the planets is dependent on the development in children of a basic sense of scale, size and distance.

7. What knowledge of astronomical bodies did children have?

The final area of interest to be explored by the research was what level of knowledge children had of astronomical bodies. Could they draw the Earth, Moon and Sun in the correct relative sizes? For instance, the English & Welsh National Curriculum expects the average 7 year old to be able to distinguish them as separate bodies. Did they know what a planet or a star was, and did they have any understanding of the sequence of the phases of the Moon? These questions were explored by the use of item 5, section B, item 3 & 4, section C and item 3, section D.

The first item simply asked children to consider that they were in a spaceship in outer space - a long way from the Earth. When they looked out of the window, they could see the Earth, Sun and Moon and the question invited them to draw what they would see. The data for the number of bodies they drew in their response is shown in Table 5.25.

	Inf-Pre %	Inf-Post %	LJ-Pre %	LJ-Post %	UJ-Pre %	UJ-Post %
Three bodies	92	94	90	87	92	95
Two bodies	6	3	3	6	5	3
1 Body	3	0	0	0	0	0
No response	0	3	6	6	3	3

Table 5.25: Percentage of children whose drawings showed one, two or three bodies.

Table 5.25 shows that the overwhelming number of responses to this question showed three separate bodies. In view of the formulation of this question, the results are hardly surprising. More interesting is the detail of their responses shown in Fig 5.19. The data collected here are for the relative sizes of the three bodies shown in the diagram.

What the data show is that the number of children who drew the Sun as being the largest body, increased for all groups as a consequence of the intervention. For both the lower and upper juniors, this change was significant (p<0.01) and only just failed to reach significance for the infants (p<0.05). These data would indicate that the concept of the Sun being a much larger astronomical body than the Earth or Moon can be assimilated by young children of all ages.

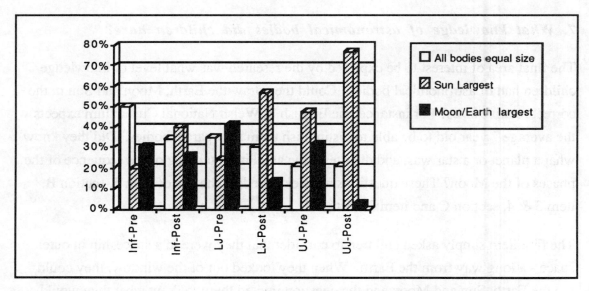

Fig 5.19: Data for relative sizes of bodies in children's drawings of the Sun, Moon and Earth from the window of a spaceship.

The next item asked children to indicate which out of the Earth, Moon, Sun, Venus, Mars, Polaris, Satellite, Scorpio, Alpha Centauri and Jupiter they thought were stars. Whilst some of this list of objects are not commonly known, the intent behind the question was to mix objects which are commonly accepted as being stars, or associated with a star, with objects which are less familiar to see how successful children were at an item which tested a knowledge of a simple factual item. This item proved difficult for many pupils and results were ultimately classified into three broad categories which were - all items correct, partially correct in that the Sun had been marked with other items and incorrect. The results are shown in Table 5.26.

	Inf-Pre %	Inf-Post %	LJ-Pre %	LJ-Post %	UJ-Pre %	UJ-Post %
Correct Response	6	14	0	19	13	51
Sun and other items marked	8	14	35	48	31	31
Incorrect	86	72	65	32	56	18

Table 5.26: Percentage of children giving one of three categories of response to question asking them to state which objects in a given list were stars.

The data show quite clearly that this is not a task which the majority of children were able to successfully complete until they were age 10/11. The intervention has had a positive effect in all cases in improving the percentage who were able to either give a correct response or at least provide a response which was partially correct. In the case of the upper juniors this change was significant at the .01 level and at the .05 level for lower juniors. In that sense, this would imply that this simple definition of a star and its exemplars can be understood by older primary age children.

A similar question was used to explore whether children had assimilated the concept of a planet. An examination of the data found that the main categories of answer were - all planets correctly indicated, some planets correctly indicated, all planets and other objects indicated and incorrect responses. The results are shown in table 5.27.

	Inf-Pre %	Inf-Post %	LJ-Pre %	LJ-Post %	UJ-Pre %	UJ-Post %
All correct	3	6	16	26	33	62
Some planets correct	39	53	29	6	23	8
All planets correctly indicated but other objects included as well	36	36	55	58	41	31
Incorrect	22	6	0	10	3	0

Table 5.27: Data for children's responses to question asking them to indicate which items in a list were planets.

The data show a similar trend to the previous question. The upper juniors were the only group to show a significant increase (p<0.05) in the number getting the answer correct but the general trend was for an improvement in the number getting a response which was totally correct. The trend is not so clear if the figures for a partially correct answer are collapsed with those for a totally correct answer. Then the percentage for infants, pre and post, is 42% to 59%, for lower juniors a decrease from 45% to 32% and for upper juniors an increase from 56% to 70% and none of these was significant. However the data do show that the idea of a planet and its definition was more fully understood by upper junior children and that this may be the appropriate age group for the introduction of this concept.

This trend is supported by the data obtained from a later item (Question 3, section D), asking children if they could explain what a star is. Answers were simply classified into serious responses containing relevant scientific aspects, those which were irrelevant and those for which no response was provided. The data are shown in Fig 5.20 and show a similar improvement in children's response with age.

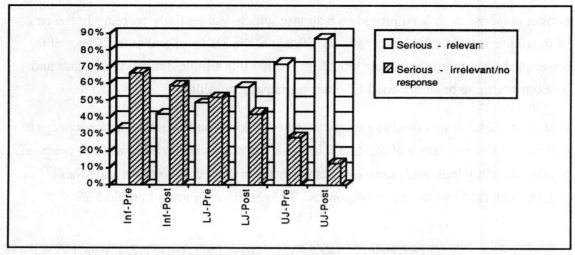

Fig 5.20: Chart showing the data for children's explanations of a star.

The second part of this question asked children to tell the interviewer the name of a star and the data for their responses are shown in Table 5.24.

	Inf-Pre %	Inf-Post %	LJ-Pre %	LJ-Post %	UJ-Pre %	UJ-Post %
Sun	0	8	16	35	31	56
Other incorrect response	36	33	42	39	31	28
Don't Know	64	58	42	26	38	15

Table 5.28: Data for children's responses when asked to provide the name of a star.

The data show that a steady improvement across all age ranges in the number of children who were able to say spontaneously that the Sun was a star. Perhaps not surprisingly, no child gave any other correct response to this question since the names of stars are not generally well-known. The data also show that the number of correct answers increased after the intervention and that the change for the upper juniors was significant ($p < 0.05$).

The final question explored whether these children were aware of the different phases of the Moon that can be observed in one month and whether they could place them in the correct sequence. A drawing of the different phases of the Moon was shown to children and they were asked to mark which of these they had previously seen. The data for their responses are shown in Figs 5.21 (a) & 5.21 (b). They were then asked which order they thought that they appeared in.

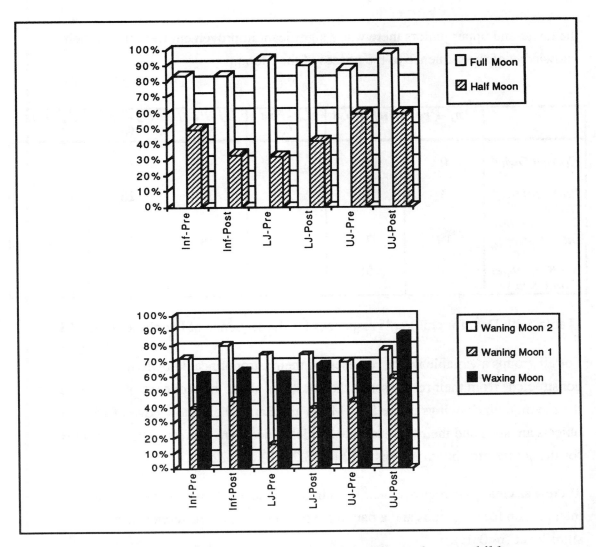

Fig 5.21 (a) & 21 (b): Chart showing which phases of moon children recognised (percentages)

The data for the results are shown above. Not surprisingly a Full Moon was recognised by the greatest percentage of children at all age levels and three phases of the Moon were recognised by more than 50% of all children. Interestingly, there seemed to be little variation across the age groups and this would suggest that most children had experienced some observation of the Moon at a relatively early age.

However the data in Table 5.29 show that only a small minority of lower and upper juniors were capable of ordering the phases of the Moon correctly. A larger number could provide a response which was partially correct in that only one item was incorrectly placed. The lack of a correct sequence is most likely indicative of a lack of any model of the cause of the phases of the Moon which enables a correct sequence to be generated. On first sight, the intervention seems to have had little effect on children's capability to answer the question correctly. However, if the correct responses are collapsed with those which show a partially correct order, then for both the lower and upper juniors there was a significant improvement (p<0.05) in their knowledge of the sequence of the phases of the Moon.

	Inf-Pre %	Inf-Post %	LJ-Pre %	LJ-Post %	UJ-Pre %	UJ-Post %
Correct Order	0	0	6	10	0	10
Part Correct Order	3	11	23	32	26	26
Incorrect	19	31	71	58	72	64
No Response/ Don't Know	78	58	0	0	3	0

Table 5.29: Data for children's responses for the sequence of the phases of the Moon.

For all groups a variable which represented their astronomical knowledge was constructed[8] from their responses to the questions about the sequence of the phases of the moon, their drawings of the Sun, Moon and Earth, their knowledge of which objects are stars and their knowledge of which objects are planets. The distributions for the scores are shown in Figs 5.22 (a), 5.22 (b) & 5.22 (c).

There was clearly an improvement in their general level of knowledge after the intervention for all groups and a paired t-test shows that the difference is highly significant (p<0.01).

---

8   This was constructed from their responses to -
   • Question 5, section B where a correct response was given double the weighting of an incorrect response;
   • Question 3, section C;
   • Question 4 (a), section C where a totally correct response was given double the weighting of a partially correct response;
   • Question 4 (b), section C where a totally correct response was given double the weighting of a partially correct response.

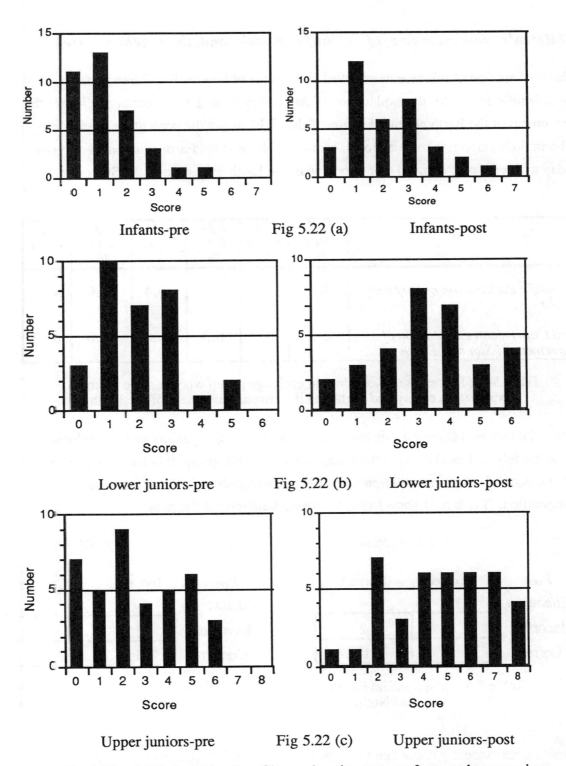

Infants-pre   Fig 5.22 (a)   Infants-post

Lower juniors-pre   Fig 5.22 (b)   Lower juniors-post

Upper juniors-pre   Fig 5.22 (c)   Upper juniors-post

Fig 5.22a, 5.22b & 5.22c: Bar Charts showing range of scores by grouping
on questions eliciting astronomical knowledge.

Children's understanding of scientific models and their general use

The final section of this research looked at the issue of how well children understood the scientific model for the explanation of day and night and the Copernican view of the movement of the Earth around the Sun. Table 5.30 shows the percentage of children who in their responses to Question 1, section D showed the Earth spun on its axis once a day and, who also showed that in one year, the Earth goes around the Sun once.

	Inf-Pre %	Inf-Post %	LJ-Pre %	LJ-Post %	UJ-Pre %	UJ-Post %
Scientific explanation of Day and Night	8.3	5.6	9.7	19.4	35.9	46.2
Full Copernican explanation of movement of Sun and Earth	8.3	6.0	0.0	25.8	44.0	69.2

Table 5.30: Percentage of children in each age group who held the scientific explanation of day and night and the annual movement of the Earth

These data show that only a substantial number of the upper juniors had assimilated these models and used them in their responses. For this group, it is interesting to see to what extent it is the same children who hold these models before and after the intervention. Table 5.31 shows simple cross-tabulations of the data.

Pre-Elicitation

Post Elicitation	Incorrect	Correct
Incorrect	19	2
Correct	6	12

Table 5.31 (a) Scientific Explanation of Day and Night

Pre-Elicitation

Post Elicitation	Incorrect	Correct
Incorrect	11	1
Correct	11	16

Table 5.31 (b): Copernican Explanation of Annual Movement of Earth

These tables evidently show that for both models, over fifty percent of the children who provided the scientific explanation for the daily and annual movements of the Sun and Earth in the pre-elicitation also provided the same models in the post-elicitation. This would suggest that once the model has been internalised and assimilated, it is relatively robust and unchangeable. Such an analysis is supported by the Del values: the value for success in providing the scientific explanation in the post-elicitation being dependent on success in providing the scientific explanation in the pre-elicitation was 0.73 and highly significant (p<0.001). The G index of agreement was +0.59 and similarly significant. The G index of agreement for the responses to the question eliciting the Copernican model was +0.38 (p<0.01) and the Del value for the interdependence of the responses was 0.81 (p<0.001) showing that success in the post-elicitation was highly dependent on success in the pre-elicitation.

Table 5.32a & 5.32b respectively show how many of the children who held the correct/incorrect scientific explanation for day and night, also held the correct/incorrect scientific explanation for the annual movement of the Earth in the pre- and post-elicitation respectively.

	Scientific Explanation for Day & Night				Scientific Explanation for Day & Night	
Copernican Explanation				Copernican Explanation		
	Incorrect	Correct			Incorrect	Correct
Incorrect	20	2		Incorrect	11	1
Correct	5	12		Correct	10	17

Table 5.32a: Pre-Elicitation   Table 5.32b: Post-Elicitation

Again, these tables show that there is a clear correlation between the children who have assimilated the scientific explanation of day and night and those who have assimilated the scientific explanation for the annual movements of the Earth. The G index of agreement was 0.64 prior to the intervention and 0.44 after the intervention. Both were highly significant (p<0.01). The Del values (0.75 pre-elicitation, 0.82 post-elicitation) also show that the development of the scientific model for day and night is dependent on success in assimilating the Copernican world view rather than the inverse.

Further cross-tabulations were used to explore to what extent pupils' abilities to explain the daily movement of the Sun (Table 5.33a & 5.33b) and to develop the scientific conception of 'down' were related to the scientific model of the daily and annual movement of the Earth (Table 5.34a & 5.34b). Since so few infants and lower juniors had successfully assimilated this model, the data have little meaning as some cells have frequencies of 0, 1 or 2 which limits any inferences which can be drawn from the statistics. Hence the data discussed here are limited to the results for upper juniors.

The G index for the relationship between the scientific model of the daily movement of the Earth and the apparent motion of the Sun were both significant in the pre- and post-elicitation (p<0.01).

		PRE		Daily Movement of the Sun	POST	
Scientific		Incorrect	Correct		Incorrect	Correct
Explanation						
for Day &	Incorrect	24	1		18	9
Night	Correct	11	3		3	9

Table 5.33 (a)   Table 5.33 (b)

Analysis of the Del coefficients shows that the significant relationship was in the post-elicitation where success in showing the correct daily movement of the Sun was a pre-condition for success in providing the scientific model of the daily movement of the Earth (Del =0.54, p<0.01).

		PRE		Scientific Concept of 'Down'	POST	
Scientific		Incorrect	Correct		Incorrect	Correct
Explanation						
for Day &	Incorrect	15	0		11	10
Night	Correct	2	12		6	12

Table 5.34 (a)   Table 5.34 (b)

Analysis of the figures shown in Table 5.34 (a) and 5.34 (b) shows that the significant relationship was in the pre-elicitation. The G index of agreement was 0.86 which is significant at p<0.01. Similarly the Del coefficients show that understanding the scientific concept of 'down' and the scientific explanation for day and night are both highly dependent on each other (Del = 0.67, p<0.001) and these two items seem to be strongly associated. However after the intervention, there was no such association. A possible explanation is that the intervention has been more successful in developing the scientific concept of 'down' than it has in improving children's understanding of why day and night happens which has resulted in a weakening of the pre-existing association.

Cross tabulations were also conducted with the data for the relationship between the Copernican world view and the latter two variables but no relationships of any significance were found. The implication of these results is that there is some evidence that, prior to the intervention, the scientific explanation of day and night is dependent on an understanding of the annual movement of the Earth and the scientific conception of 'down'. After the intervention, whilst this understanding was still dependent on a knowledge of the annual movement of the Sun, it was now contingent on a knowledge of the daily trajectory of the Sun across the sky.

Further exploration of the data showed that the development of the Copernican world view would appear to have happened for these children in a holistic matter. There were very few children who had assimilated separately the information or idea that the Earth moves or that it moves around the Sun once. Children either understood and articulated both of these pieces of information in their response or neither.

Finally there were no significant G indexes of agreement between children's choices for the shape of the Earth and their responses which indicated that they had understood the scientific concept of 'down'. These results would support the argument that these two ideas are seen by children as being unrelated, and that in choosing a shape for the Earth, they do not necessarily conceive of it as the ground on which they live.

6. Conclusions

The picture that emerges from this study is one in which children's knowledge of astronomical events seems to be in a process of development across the age range. Additionally, in many instances, the intervention has had a positive effect in improving their knowledge and understanding. An essential question for consideration is whether this progress represents a coherent change to any theory-like structures that children may be using or, whether alternatively, it is better characterised by simple improvements in pieces of unrelated knowledge which are essentially of a figural nature. Typically such knowledge is highly context dependent and characterised by a symbolic representation which corresponds closely to the phenomenon itself.

Evidence for the improvement in their understanding can be found by examining the compound variable for their astronomical knowledge (Fig 5.22a, 5.22b & 5.22c) and table 6.1 shows the data for their mean scores and table 6.2 the data for the standard deviations.

	Pre	Post
Infants	1.31	2.31
Lower Juniors	3.00	3.29
Upper Juniors	2.64	4.61

Table 6.1: Average scores achieved on items eliciting astronomical knowledge.

The apparent anomaly in these data is the higher score of the lower juniors in the pre-elicitation for which there is no evident explanation. This data were collected from two groups of children in different schools and it is possible that they had undertaken some study of astronomy previously. However, after the intervention, the improvement in their scores was again correlated with age which is suggestive of a developmental progression.

	Pre	Post
Infants	1.31	1.68
Lower Juniors	1.31	1.69
Upper Juniors	1.93	2.14

Table 6.2: Standard deviations for the average scores on items eliciting astronomical knowledge.

Interestingly, these data for the standard deviations show that, whilst there is an overall improvement in the level of their knowledge, it is accompanied by an increasing spread and greater diversity.

The general trend of improving astronomical knowledge can be found elsewhere in the data. Fig 5.11 shows more children giving the Copernican account of the annual movement of the Sun and Earth as they get older, and that this trend is enhanced by the effect of the intervention. Similar trends are also found in their explanations for day and night as Fig 5.12a shows an increase across the age range in the number of children who stated that night was accounted for by the spin of the Earth rather than the movement of the Sun. The trend is confirmed by the data in Fig 5.14 and table 5.30 which show a similar pattern in the number of children giving this explanation with models for day and night. Again, the percentage of children correctly showing the position and length of a shadow at midday (Table 5.18) and the height of the midday sun (Fig 5.16a), also showed a trend of improvement with age in children's knowledge.

A similar but less marked trend exists in the data for children's understanding of the Earth concept with more older children succeeding in providing the scientific response (Fig 5.18) which showed that they held the idea that 'down' lay in a direction towards the centre of the Earth.

Children's understanding of distance was essentially weak although a sizeable minority do seem capable of operating with a relative sense of scale in sorting operations. The intervention only had a marginal positive effect on their achievements on these tasks and this suggests that there is substantial difficulty for young children in grasping a feel for the scale associated with standard measurements of distance. These data also call into question whether children of this age can grasp the enormity of the Solar System in comparison to the dimensions of their own daily world.

In all of these data, it should also be noted that the effects of the intervention were positive. The lack of any control group inevitably means that the claim cannot be advanced that this is a more effective method of improving children's understanding than others, but it does show that such a pedagogical approach does have efficacy in achieving some of its aims.

Not surprisingly, older children were also found to have a better understanding of the units and interrelationships of time (Figs 5.4, 5.5 and 5.6). What is more, a closer analysis of these data shows that its development is correlated, with success on one item strongly linked to success on another item (Figs 5.7a, 5.7b & 5.7c). Hence the picture presented by the data is one in which the growth of the concept of time is something unitary and holistic rather than an assemblage of independent pieces of knowledge.

However, such a coherent growth in children's understanding is not presented by other aspects of the data where children's thinking appears to be fragmented and unrelated. Surprisingly, their knowledge of the daily trajectory of the Sun across the sky was poor with a maximum of 31% of upper junior children after the intervention being capable of showing the correct height and correct sequence of movement for the morning, midday and afternoon positions of the Sun. Only for the upper juniors, after the intervention, was there any indication that this knowledge was correlated with their ability to predict the length and position of a shadow at midday and even then, this just failed to be significant. The implication is that these items are seen as separate and discrete and only some of the older children are beginning to see these phenomena as connected.

More evidence for children's knowledge being discrete is provided by the data in Tables 5.9 (a) and 5.9 (b). These show that there was no association between i) children's knowledge of the variation of altitude of the Sun between summer/winter and the length of the day, or ii) children's knowledge of the variation of altitude of the Sun between summer/winter and seasonal variations in temperature apart from the first relationship for lower juniors before the intervention. In many cases the correlations were negative and this reinforces the picture that such knowledge is fragmented and lacks a coherent, unitary picture in the child's mind.

Similarly exploring any relationships that might exist between children's knowledge of the daily movement and variation of the height of the Sun and the change in shadow length, no correlations were found apart from one. That was, that for infants and upper juniors prior to the intervention, but not lower juniors, knowledge of a shorter shadow at midday was a precondition for being able to explain how to use the sundial for measuring time. This relationship persisted for infants after the intervention.

Finally, no correlations were found between the shapes that children chose for the shape of the Earth and the responses for the direction of fall of a ball at three points on the surface of the Earth though the response for upper juniors after the intervention approached significance.

The lack of any clear network of connections between these separate items suggests strongly that such knowledge is purely figural i.e. that it is seen as independent and unrelated by the child who is unable to operate and generate the abstract relationships that exist e.g. that an increased elevation of the Sun above the horizon will result in the Sun's rays hitting the earth at a more acute angle which will foreshorten the shadow. Thus such data call into question Vosniadou's assertion[1] that children are consistently using one model to explain a range of astronomical phenomena. However, there is some support for her statement that the key to conceptual understanding is the development of the scientific concept of 'down' from the responses of the upper juniors. Analysis of table 5.32a shows success in comprehending this idea was a pre-condition for acquiring the scientific explanation for day and night *in the pre-elicitation,* where children's understanding was explored prior to any study of astronomy, effectively similar conditions to Vosniadou's research.

However, after the intervention, this dependence was weakened and no longer significant. A possible interpretation of this change is that the relationship is initially crucial for the development of the scientific world view but the link weakens with enhanced domain-specific knowledge.

Implications for the National Curriculum.

One of the secondary aims of this research was to explore to what extent the attainment targets of the English and Welsh national curriculum represented a realistic set of goals that could be achieved by the majority of children of the intended age and ability. These levels of attainment were essentially formulated by an empirical process using the professional judgements of a body of science educators. Yet there is little research that has been undertaken in this domain that would support or confirm their judgements. What light do these data cast on the validity of the targets as measuring instruments of children's attainment?

The glaring inconsistency that emerges is that the most basic level 1 requirement that children should be able to describe the apparent motion of the Sun across the sky is only achievable by a maximum of 31% of *upper juniors* after the intervention. Whilst there is nothing intrinsically difficult about this piece of knowledge as it is a concrete observable fact, it does show that the majority of children are not aware of the Sun's

---

1   Vosniadou, S. (1991) Conceptual Development in Astronomy in Glynn, S. M, Yeany, R. H. & Britton, B. K. (Eds) *The Psychology of Learning Science.* New Jersey: Lawrence Erlbaum.

trajectory across the horizon and that exercises need to be undertaken to specifically draw the phenomenon to their attention. Even then, the data reported in this study question whether the idea is easily assimilated and suggest that it will only be acquired as an isolated fact.

In contrast, the level 2 requirement that children know that the Earth, Moon and Sun are separate spherical bodies seems to be easily achievable. Over two thirds of all children at any age selected a sphere for the shape of the Earth (Table 5.20) and over 90% of all children drew three bodies when asked to draw the Earth, Sun and Moon as seen from the window of a spaceship. The variation in facility between these two items would suggest that the order of the statements of attainment at level 1 and 2 is inappropriate and should at least be reversed.

The level 3 statement requires children to show that the appearance of the Moon and the altitude of the Sun change in a regular and predictable manner. In that 50% of all children were capable of recognising at least three phases of the Moon, there is some evidence to suggest that this target may be attainable. However, some doubt is cast on this assertion by the fact that only a maximum of 42% of upper juniors were capable of placing these phases in the correct order. Data have already been presented to show that children's knowledge of the daily movement of the Sun was weak and only a maximum of 32% of lower juniors and 23% of upper juniors were able to correctly show the difference in altitude between the summer and winter Sun. Taken together, this would suggest that only a minority of even upper junior children, age 11, would be capable of attaining this level which is supposed to be achievable by the average child of this age.

The level 4 statement requires children to be able to explain day and night, the length of the day and year in terms of the movement of the Earth around the Sun. Table 5.30 shows that 69% of upper junior children were capable of giving the Copernican explanation for the annual movement of the Sun after the intervention. However, only 46% of upper children provided the scientific explanation for day and night even after the intervention. However, such data would support the notion that the average child should be capable of attaining such a level.

The level 5 statement requires children to be able to describe the motion of the planets in the solar system. Since this attainment target was introduced to the second version of the national curriculum, after the research had begun, this aspect of children's knowledge was not explored.

Clearly these data show that there is some inconsistency in the difficulty of the levels of attainment and, as a representation of a developmental scale, they may currently be at best inaccurate or at worst seriously flawed. Such research should therefore encourage teachers to regard the detail of the framework of the national curriculum for this topic with a healthy scepticism until it reflects more accurately research of this nature. It is our belief that the data reported here show more definitively what is a reasonable expectation of children's astronomical knowledge from age 5 to 11. In the meantime, teachers would be advised to give more credence to the broad outline of entitlement embodied in the programme of study at each key stage.

This research has attempted to maintain ecological validity by basing itself firmly in the classroom, using a range of accessible and simple intervention strategies over the time scale often allocated to a topic within schools. The gains reported are a reflection of what improvement in understanding is achievable in this context, typically over a half term period. What is missing from this picture is any indication of what might be feasible for children's understanding by adopting such a pedagogic process over a more extended period of several years. It is hoped that a sustained emphasis on discussion and reflection would encourage the growth of a coherent understanding rather than the assimilation of individual fragments of knowledge. Only further research will tell.

Appendix 1: Schools

ILEA

Inspector for Science Education   John Wray

Schools

Ashmole Primary	Lambeth
St Edwards Roman Catholic School	Newham
Brampton Primary School	Newham
Culloden Primary School	Tower Hamlets
Summerside Primary School	Barnet
Altmore Infants School	Newham
Henry Fawcett Junior	Lambeth
Rhyl Primary	Camden
Benthal Primary	Hackney
Joseph Lancaster Primary	Southwark

Appendix 2 : Elicitation Questions

Section A

1   a How long is a day?

     b How long is a month?

     c How long is a year?

2. Add to this picture to show, if you were looking towards the south, where the sun would be:-

    a in the early morning
    b in the middle of the day
    c in the afternoon.

    d. What happens to the Sun throughout the day?

3.   a. What happens to the sun at night?

      b. Can you explain (tell me) why night happens?

Section B

1. How is a summer day different from a winter day? Can you think of three differences?

2. Here is a picture of a playground, you are looking towards the sun and it is the middle of the day.

   Can you add to the picture to show where the Sun would be in winter (W) and in summer (S).

3. Here is a picture showing a tree and its shadow early in the morning.

   a Can you add to the picture to show where the shadow would be in the middle of the day?

   Use this space to explain (tell me about) your drawing.

4. Do you know how shadows can be used to help us tell the time?

5. a Here are 5 drawings. Which ones have you seen the moon look like?

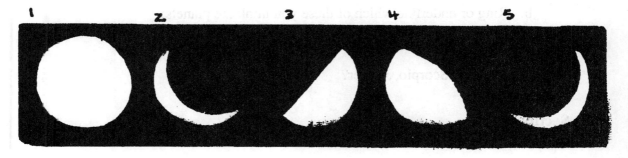

   b (If more than two identified) Can you show me which one you would start with, which is second and so on?

Section C

1   Look at this set of shapes.

    a   Which one do you think is shaped most like the Earth?

    b.   Can you explain (tell me) why you think the Earth is shaped like that?

2.   This drawing shows three people on different parts of the world. They are all holding a stone. Mark on the drawing how the stone will move when they let go of it.

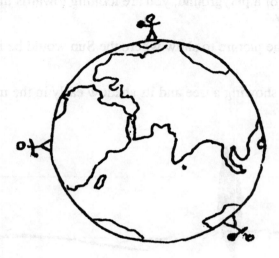

3.   Imagine you are in a spaceship in outer space. You look out of the window; how would you see the Sun, Moon and Earth?

    a   Use this space to draw what you would see.

    b   Tell me about your drawing.

4   a.   Ring or underline which of these you think are stars:-

    Earth, Moon, Sun, Venus, Mars, Polaris,

    Satellite, Scorpio, Alpha Centauri, Jupiter?

    b.   Ring or underline which of these you think are planets:-

    Earth, Moon, Sun, Venus, Mars, Polaris,

    Satellite, Scorpio, Jupiter?

Section D

1   a.   Choose two shapes from this set to represent the Sun and the Earth.

b. Can you show me what happens in one day and night?

(I'll hold one for you; which one would you like me to hold? If you want me to move mine, tell me how to move it.)

c. *(if child has given an answer to b. above)* Can you show me what happens during one year?

2*   Using the shapes or by drawing, can you explain (tell me):

a. Why days are longer in summer?

b. Why it is hotter in summer than in winter?

3.   a. Can you explain (tell me) what a star is?

b. Can you tell me one?

4*. Look at the set of 6 cards about distances. Can you put them in the right order, starting with the largest?

Can you tell me how far it is from London to:-

a. New York
b. The Sun
c. Margate (Southend)
d. The Moon
e. Mars
f. Liverpool

5*. Look at the set of 6 cards about parts of the Solar System (Sun, Moon, Earth, Jupiter, Mars, Saturn)

a. Can you put them in order of size starting from the largest?

b. Can you write each name in this table, starting with the largest and write how big you think they are?

	Part of the Solar System	How big are they?
a.		
b.		
c.		
d.		
e.		
f.		

---

*   These questions were not used with infant children

Appendix 3: Intervention Activities

This appendix contains the notes that were provided to teachers for the intervention activities. In the briefing given to teachers, emphasis was placed on using a range of these strategies in any order that suited their work. Teachers were asked to select activities that they considered appropriate to the child's understanding and encourage them to explore their understanding and thinking of the relevant concept further.

1. Time lines

This activity aims to encourage children to think about themselves and their lives as a series of events related in time. Many of the concepts associated with Earth in Space depend upon the pupils having some idea about time, from length of days and nights to ideas about months and lunar cycles to understandings of years and the seasonal changes that occur during a year.

Description

For all ages from 5 to 11 years - make a time line for a short period, initially a day, in which to record some information about memorable activities and events and times at which they happen. For infant pupils, this could be done without mention of clock time, but with reference to major breaks in the day e.g.:-

Leave home - arrive at school - first play - lunch - home time - playcentre - bed time.......

For older children, develop this into a time strip or time line covering longer periods e.g. a week, a month or a year showing events in order and dates. This could be developed further into a time strip for the whole of a child's life. A sample strip is shown beneath. Children add events to the boxes, either as pictures or in writing.

Monday	Tues	Wed	Thurs	Fri	Sat	Sun

Timeline for a week

The activity involves drawing a line or producing a strip chart. One end represents the beginning of the period being studied and the other the finish. Children then mark on the chart events in their relative position. So a chart for the year could have Christmas, my birthday, holidays, sister's or brother's birthdays on.

This activity or something similar is important in that preliminary findings show that infant children have little understanding of the adult's segmentation of time.

Follow up ideas

Using 24 hour clock and pie charts of daily happenings.
Make a time line of some famous person in History (a Scientist?).

2. Discussion Activity

Explanation

The following activity is designed to encourage children to reflect on their own explanations for astronomical phenomena.

Description

Give the children a set of cards. Each card should have on it one of the following statements.

'The Sun goes to bed at night.'

'The Sun hides behind the clouds at night'

'The Sun goes beneath the earth at night'

'The Sun goes round to the other side at night'

'The Sun does not move. The earth does and we turn away from the Sun at night.'

'The moon shines because light from the Sun bounces off it.'

'The moon shines because it has its own light like a light bulb.'

(and any other statements that would be relevant)

For each statement, children should be asked to work in a group, stating whether they agree or disagree. They should also be asked how they know what they think is right and to record their evidence.

3. Directed Reading Activities

Explanation

Much of the information about the Earth and the Solar System has to come from secondary sources e.g. teachers, parents and books as it it impossible to investigate some of the ideas being introduced here. Whilst books are valuable, the act of reading for information (reflective reading) as opposed to reading for enjoyment (receptive reading) can be encouraged by the use of directed reading activities which force children to return to a passage and extract information from it. Appendix 1 & 2 include some examples which can be used with children who are capable of reading i.e. lower and upper juniors.

Description

Give out the passages and ask the pupils to follow the instructions at the end.

Follow up activities

It is very easy to develop more of the Cloze procedure reading activities by using the computer program TRAY or similar programs. The text has to be typed in and children then buy letters and attempt to reveal the text. This forces them to think about the text and its factual content.

4. Shapes

Explanation

Many children have difficulty in describing the shapes of the Earth, Sun and Moon. This activity is intended to familiarise the pupils with a variety of 2 and 3 dimensional shapes, extend their powers of observation, enhance their vocabulary and make it easier for them to recognise and describe shapes.

Description

Collect a set of flat and three dimensional shapes, but mainly ones with round edges. Children should work in groups. One child should be given the shapes, either in a dark 'feely bag' or asked to take them behind a screen so that the other child cannot see them. The child with the shapes is then asked to describe the shapes and the rest of the group should attempt to guess which one of the following shapes it is e.g. a sphere, cylinder, disc, circle, rectangle, block or cuboid.

The group doing the asking can ask questions like:
- How many sides has it?
- How many edges and corners?
- Where have you seen shapes like this?
- How would you describe the shape to somebody over the telephone?
- With younger children, use a feely box so they can try to describe the shape which they can feel, but which is hidden from the others. Other feely box activities might include:
- Put four shapes into the box and provide a larger collection visible to the child. Ask the child to feel a hidden shape and then choose the visible shape which is the same.
- Ask the child to name, as accurately as possible, the hidden shape.
- Organise a group of children to ask ten questions of the child who is feeling the hidden shape, to see if they can identify it without looking at it.

Follow up ideas

With older children identify shapes in the environment and try to link shape to function. Attempt some mathematical classification of shapes which may describe the numbers of sides, edges and corners. Differentiate between the various "round" shapes, so that pupils begin to use more accurate descriptions like disc, circle, cylinder, sphere.

5. Scrap books

Explanation

Children need to relate the ideas about science they learn in school with the many influences they receive from the media. Collecting pictures and other items from magazines and newspapers will encourage them to think about how the ideas they are developing are used in the media and to help them to make sense of the impressions they receive.

Description

Collect magazines and newspapers. Ask the pupils to find and cut out pictures which show daytime or night-time, the Sun or sunsets or sunrises, moon, stars and planets. Ask them to stick these pictures into a large scrap book with some brief comments from the children. Scrap books could be a class scrapbook, a group scrapbook or individual ones. These scrapbooks can be used with infants as a stimulus for discussions in class or groups and with older children to stimulate investigations or writing about the Earth in Space.

Follow up ideas

Pupils can be encouraged to prepare their own books, using a variety of materials from magazines and their own drawings and written comments. Pupils might include in their own books information taken from other sources and present it in their own ways, e.g. charts on solar system information.

6. Draw an object

Explanation

This activity is intended to encourage children to imagine things from other people's viewpoint as well as to observe things closely from their own perspective. Children often find it very difficult to lose their egocentric ideas and appreciate that things may appear different if you observe them from a different place. An example of this is the apparent movement of the Sun across the sky. The Sun appears to rise in the East and set in the West, whereas really what is happening is that the Earth is spinning and the Sun is still in relation to the Earth.

Description

Egocentric viewpoints - for younger children, ask pupils to sit in a circle round an object and draw what they see. Then compare the different drawings. Suitable objects for this exercise would be things which do appear different from various angles. A teapot might be suitable in this activity.

For older pupils, then try to imagine what it would look like from another child's position - draw it from the other viewpoint.

This activity can then be used with a torch shone onto a spherical shape which represents a globe. Children can be seated around the globe and asked to draw what the globe looks like from their position. (The crosses mark positions in which the children can be placed.)

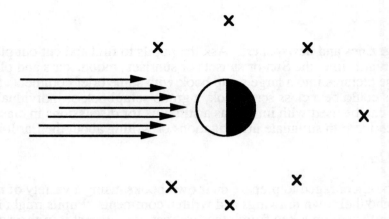

7. Ordering the planets

This activity is designed to give the children a sense of the size and distance of the planets.

Description

Produce a set of cards, each with the name of a planet on it. Ask the children to use books to find out which is the largest, the next largest and so on so that they can put them in an order which corresponds to their size.

Then repeat the activity and ask them to place them in order of distance from the Sun.

Finally you can take them out into the playground and show them the scale of the distances.

Planet	Distance From Sun (millions of km)	Distance Across Playground metre
(Sun)	0	0.0
Mercury	58	0.4
Venus	108	0.7
Earth	150	1.0
Mars	227	1.5
Jupiter	748	5.2
Saturn	1425	9.5
Uranus	2869	19.0
Neptune	4490	30.0
Pluto	5837	39.0

If the playground is not large enough, the distances can be halved.
Taking a photograph is a useful way of recording the event.

8. Estimating sizes

Explanation

We want children to have some idea about the size and scale of the Solar System. Things which are near appear larger than things which are further away. This activity aims at making this more apparent to pupils. To understand that the Sun is a star (level 4) you need to understand that some things look large because they are nearer.

Description

Organise the children into small groups of six or seven. One child is the observer who stands at the front and the other children then distribute themselves about the room or the playground. The child at the front is asked to work out 'Who is the tallest?' and 'Who is the smallest?' without moving either themselves or any of the other children.

You can suggest that they try using their thumb for sighting purposes. However in reality, this challenge is impossible as you have to know how far away are the objects. Do not tell the children this but see if they can arrive at this conclusion themselves.

Then ask one child to be the Sun. This child should be placed very close to the observer. All the other children are stars and go as far away as possible. The child at the front then has to say whether

a) 'the Sun' and 'the Stars' look very different in size.
b) Whether they really are the same size and if so why do they appear to be different sizes?

Ask the children all to take turns at being the observer at the front. Their experience can then be used as a basis for discussing whether the Sun could be a star.

9. Other people's ideas

Explanation

By presenting children with the ideas of others, we want to help them compare their own ideas and see whether their ideas match up in explanatory power.

Description

Prepare a list of alternative views about the Earth in Space, which may arise either from historical and mythical ideas, or from the ideas of the pupils within the class. Present these to groups of children and ask them to discuss and come to some consensus about their own ideas on the issue. They should be asked to suggest how they could find some evidence to back up their thinking. Some suggestions for starting points:-

"Some people think the Earth is a flat shape, others think it is spherical."

"Some people think the Earth goes round the Sun each day, others think the Earth goes round the Sun once every year."

"Some people think the earth goes round the Sun, others that the Sun goes round the Earth."

"The ancient Greeks believed that the Sun was a chariot of fire, driven across the sky each day whilst the Egyptians thought the Sun was carried away at night on a boat to the other side of the earth."

10. Seasonal change

Explanation

This activity is intended to encourage children to notice and respond to seasonal changes through drawing, writing, painting, drama, etc.

Description

This is a sorting activity which encourages children to think about changes that occur from season to season. Give the children the following statements cut up as thin strips and then ask them to order them into groups. Let the children devise their own groups.

The days are hot	It gets dark at 4 o'clock
Daffodils are out	We go on our holidays
Snow falls	The leaves fall
Blossom is out	Birds leave for other countries
Roses are out	The days are cold
Lots of rain falls	The days are very short
The wind blows strongly	The Sun is high in the sky
The Sun is low in the sky	It is dark when I get up
Flowers are growing	Lambs are in the fields

When the children have finished they can compare theirs with other groups.

Using the tables of temperatures in major cities, they can be asked if it is hot everywhere at the same time. Ask the children to produce three groups (possibly upper juniors only).

Places the same temperature   Places that are hotter   Places that are cooler

What pattern is there to the cities that are in the last two groups?

Finally children can then be asked to consider 'What causes the seasons?' Ask the children to see if they can find out or think of reasons why it gets hotter in the summer. Responses that say that it is because we get closer to the Sun can be challenged by saying that that does not explain why the Sun gets higher in the sky in summer.

11. Log books

Explanation

A log book is something used by the pupils to make records of things that they observe over a period of time. They are also used by children to record their ideas about what they observe. Ideally, the entries in log books should be dated, so that the time periods are recorded. Log books are intended to be used both at school and at home.

Description

A suitable sized book, with unlined pages can be made for each child. Decisions about headings also need to be made - such headings might include:-

Moon watching - draw up a chart to show the position and shape of the Moon over a month. A chart is provided at the back.

Sun and shadows - record the position of the Sun in the morning, the time it gets dark at night

Other topics that could be included are exploration of space, the stars, poems about weather and seasons, other people's ideas about the Earth in Space, etc.

Follow up ideas

Some pupils might wish to extend their log book into a well presented topic book about the theme, rewriting and redrafting their initial entries and improving their presentation. They might attempt to describe some of the investigations they carry out without the direct supervision of teachers as well as the results of their own reading of information books. Conversations with family and friends outside school could also be recorded.

12. Sundials and shadows

Explanation

Much of the work involving the Sun and shadows can be followed up within the classroom using torches and objects which form shadows. Children should be encouraged to test out the ideas they have begun to form, through early observations of the position of the Sun in the sky and the lengths and positions of shadows.

Description

Children will need to make a simple sundial. This can simply be a stick in a plant pot. This can then be placed in the play ground and children can then mark the position and length of the shadow through the day.

This sundial can then be used on the next day to measure the time.

Children can also cut strips of tape to the length of the shadow during the day at regular intervals. These strips can then be made into a chart with one placed for each hour. If they missed one hour, they will have to leave a gap. This should give a good visual picture of the change in the length of the shadow through the day.

Follow up activities

A darkened area will be needed - this can be made in a shaded part of many classrooms, with careful positioning of screens and room dividers. A variety of small objects, figures, toy animals, models from the Lego box, etc. can be used. A torch can be used to simulate the Sun in different positions. Shadows are then observed, in terms of their length for different inclinations of the "Sun" and their positions at different angles of the "Sun". It might be simpler to start with the torch, object and screen (for showing the shadow more clearly) at the same heights, and moving the torch left or right to see which way the shadow moves. Then one might position the torch at different heights and examine the length of the shadows. Finally, one might attempt to combine both inclination and angle to simulate the apparent movement of the Sun across the sky.

13. Models of Sun, Moon and Earth

Explanation

In order to help children express their ideas about the relative movements of the Sun, Moon and Earth, it is useful to get them to act out such movements and then discuss their thoughts with each other.

Description

Pupils act out the movements of Earth around Sun and Moon around Earth, including spin and orbit. Children are asked to work in pairs. One child acts as the Sun and one child acts as the Earth. Children are asked to take it in turns directing the other and show each other how they think.

a) The Earth and Sun move in a day
b) The Earth and Sun move in a year.

After a pair has finished they could join with another pair and see if they agree.

Follow up ideas

One child acts as the Moon and the other acts as the Earth. The children are then asked to show each other how they move over 28 days. (The correct answer is the the Earth should stay still and the Moon should move around once with its face pointing at the Earth all the time.)

14. Observing the Moon

This activity should encourage children to look at the night sky and make regular observations. The final charts can be compared or included in their scrap books.

Description

Provide the children with a copy of the chart and ask them to draw the Moon as they see it each night. If it is cloudy, they should record cloudy in the box.

Reading Activity 1

The system is made up of the Sun and all the objects that _____ _____ the Sun. The planets are the largest bodies that revolve around the Sun. The Earth is one of the nine known planets.

Planets are shaped like a ____ and move around the Sun. All the planets revolve around the Sun in the same direction. The path that a planet takes is called an ____. It takes _____ _____ for the earth to revolve around the Sun.

Mercury, the planet _____ to the Sun, moves completely around the Sun every 88 days. Because it is closer to the Sun than the other planets, it does not travel as many miles to complete its orbit. It does not need very much time to complete one _____.

Pluto, the planet furthest from the Sun, takes about 250 years to complete one orbit.

Planets have objects which go round them called satellites. The moon is a _____ of the Earth. Many of the planets have more than one _____. Other planets have none.

Planets do not give off _____ on their own. Like the moon, planets _____ light from the Sun. When you see a planet, you see the sunlight which is being reflected to you.

Instructions

Work in threes

1. Read through the passage.
2. Talk about what words could go in the blanks and fill in the words when you agree.
3. Underline all the words you do not understand.
4. Double underline all the words that tell you something about planets.
5. Make a list of all the words that are to do with moving.

Reading Activity 2

The _____ travels around the Sun. It takes ___ _____ to go all the way
around. This picture shows the path which the _____ takes as it travels
around the Sun.

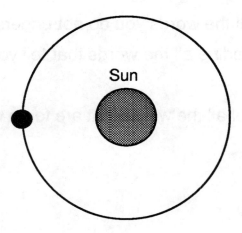

The Earth is ___ million kilometres away from the Sun. While the Earth
is travelling around the Sun it is also _____ _____ like a top. It turns
around ____ every __ hours.

The Sun can only shine on ___ ____ of the Earth at a time. It is daytime
for that side of the Earth. The side of the Earth away from the Sun is in
darkness. It is ____-_____ there. As the Earth spins around, the dark side
gradually turns to face the Sun.

As our side of the Earth turns towards the Sun we begin to see the light
from the Sun. We say that the Sun is _____. As we turn away from the
Sun, the Sun seems to go _____ in the sky. We say that the Sun is
_____.

Instructions

Work in threes

1. Read through the passage.

2. Talk about what words could go in the blanks and fill in the words when you agree.

3. Underline all the words you do not understand.

Reading Activity 3

The Sun and its planets together are called the **Solar System.** The Sun's nine planets are Mercury, Venus, Earth, Mars, Jupiter, Saturn, Uranus, Neptune and Pluto.

Mercury is the planet nearest to the Sun and Neptune and Pluto are furthest away. The planets are named after ancient Greek and Roman gods.

Mercury

Mercury travels around the Sun faster than any other planet. It takes 88 days. It was named after Mercury, who was the messenger of the gods.

Mercury is the smallest planet; it does not have any satellites. It is 58 million kilometres from the Sun. It spins around slowly, taking 59 days to turn round once. The side of the planet which faces the Sun is very hot, and the other side is very cold. It is much too hot and cold for anyone like us to live there. There is no atmosphere on Mercury as the Sun has boiled all the gases off.

Venus

Venus is a little smaller than the Earth and is 108 million kilometres away from the Sun. It shines very brightly in the sky and can be seen clearly with a telescope, sometimes even during the day. Venus was named after a Roman goddess.

Venus can never be seen very late at night. It is nearer to the Sun than we are, so when we turn away from the Sun we begin to turn away from Venus too. It is best seen in the early evening just after the Sun has set or early in the morning before dawn, and is often called 'the evening star' or the 'morning star'. It takes Venus 243 days to spin around once.

Venus is covered in a thick layer of clouds. They are not like our clouds. The clouds around Venus are made mainly of carbon dioxide, and it is impossible for us to breathe on Venus. Because of these thick clouds no one can see the surface of Venus.

Mars

Mars is smaller than the Earth and is 227 million kilometres away from the Sun. It takes Mars 687 days to travel around the Sun and just over 24 hours to spin round once.

It is easy to see the surface of Mars through a telescope because there are no clouds to hide it. Most of Mars is covered with sand and red rock and because of this it shines brightly in the night sky. This is why it is often called the 'red planet' and people think it looks angry. On Mars, dust makes the sky salmon pink in colour.

Jupiter is the next planet away from Mars.

Jupiter

Jupiter is the biggest planet. It is bigger than all the other planets put together and shines very brightly in the night sky. It was named after

Jupiter, the King of the gods. It is 748 million kilometres from the Sun and takes nearly 11 years to go round it once.

It is very cold on Jupiter. Poisonous gases swirl around it; the gases are ammonia and methane, and they look like coloured bands around the planet as it spins around. Jupiter spins around once every 10 hours. On one band there is a big, red spot. This spot was first seen in 1875, and its brightness changes from year to year. No one knows what the 'great red spot' of Jupiter really is but they think it is rather like a hurricane on Earth.

Saturn

Saturn looks beautiful through a telescope as it is surrounded by rings. Saturn was named after the Roman god of agriculture. It is smaller than Jupiter, but still very much bigger than Earth. It is 1,425 million kilometres from the Sun.

The rings around Saturn are made up of millions of pieces of rock and ice. They move round Saturn very quickly. Saturn spins around once every 10 hours. Saturn has many moons that spin around it.

Activities

1.   Make a chart which will tell you many of the facts about planets that are in the piece you have just read. Your chart should have the planets down the side and headings at the top.

Working in groups, discuss what other information you would like to put in the boxes at the top.

Now read the passage again, underlining the information for each group you have. Use a different colour for each group.

What we know about Planets

	distance from the Sun
Mercury	
Venus	
Earth	
Mars	
Jupiter	
Saturn	
Uranus	
Neptune	
Pluto	

You will have to find the information about Uranus, Neptune and Pluto from books

2.   Pretend that you are in a spaceship on your way to Venus. Your spaceship gradually gets closer and closer to the planet. It enters the thick

clouds around Venus and comes nearer to the surface of the planet. You are the first person to ever see what Venus is really like.

Write down what you would say to people on Earth through your radio. Tell them what you see and how you feel.

The Moon at Night

	Monday	Tuesday	Weds	Thurs	Fri	Sat	Sun
Week 1							
Week 2							
Week 3							
Week 4